B. Stephans.

# THE HARPS OF GOD

D

½  1  ¾  ¾  ¾  4  5

Miles

# The Harps of God

AND I SAW AS IT WERE A SEA OF GLASS MINGLED WITH FIRE:
AND THEM THAT HAD GOTTEN THE VICTORY OVER THE BEAST,
AND OVER HIS IMAGE, AND OVER HIS MARK, *AND* OVER THE
NUMBER OF HIS NAME, STAND ON THE SEA OF GLASS, HAVING
THE HARPS OF GOD.

The Book of Revelation, 15:2

by
**Kent Stetson**

**Playwrights Canada Press**
**Toronto • Canada**

**Playwrights Canada Press**
54 Wolseley St., 2nd fl.  Toronto, Ontario  CANADA M5T 1A5
Tel: (416) 703-0201    Fax: (416) 703-0059
info@puc.ca    http://www.puc.ca

Playwrights Canada Press publishes with the generous assistance of The Canada Council for the Arts – Writing and Publishing Section and the Ontario Arts Council.

ONTARIO ARTS COUNCIL
CONSEIL DES ARTS DE L'ONTARIO

Cover photo: "Disaster on Ice". The Cassie Brown Collection, COLL-115, 16.04.060, Centre for Newfoundland Studies Archives, Memorial University of Newfoundland. Inside photos: Map – Sealing Disaster 1914. GN6 WBK2, GN6 CWG1 & A42-138. Copyright of the Provincial Archives of Newfoundland and Labrador.

Production manager: Jodi Armstrong.

**National Library of Canada Cataloguing in Publication Data**

Stetson, Kent, 1948-
  Harps of God

ISBN 0-88754-606-4

I. Title.

PS8557.T465H37  2001          C812'.54          C00-932028-8
PR9199.3.S84H37  2001

First edition: July 2001.
Second printing: January 2002.
Printed and bound by AGMV Marquis at Quebec, Canada.

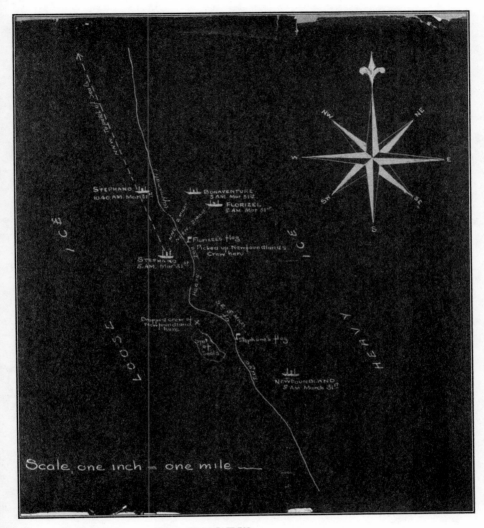

*Map – Sealing Disaster 1914. GN6 WBK2*

*Le corps humain cache notre réalité, le réalité c'est l'âme.*
Victor Hugo

# TABLE OF CONTENTS

*ii*

## DEDICATION

*The Harps of God* is dedicated,
with love and thanks, to my father
CECIL G. STETSON
on the occasion of his seventy-fifth birthday,
January 7, 1995.

## AUTHOR'S ACKNOWLEDGMENTS

In April 1994, Donna Butt, Artistic Director of Rising Tide Theatre in St. John's, Newfoundland, Canada, commissioned an original work for the stage arising from survivor's statements sworn before two commissions of inquiry into facts surrounding the Great Newfoundland Sealing Disaster of 1914. Rising Tide Theatre, The Canadian Stage Company and The National Arts Centre supported the major development of the work. A grant from Le Conseil des Arts et des Lettres du Québec supported the research and writing of the first draft of *The Harps of God*. The National Theatre School, through its resident playwright program, and the National Film Board of Canada participated in the play's development. The Centre for Newfoundland Studies, and the Provincial Archives of Newfoundland and Labrador provided assistance. I am particularly grateful to Donna Butt, Rick Boland, Bob Baker, Andes Celms, Candace Burley, Richard Rose, Bill Glassco and Gil Osborne for their thoughtful, challenging dramaturgy, and to Charles Paul Boucher for his sharp eye and full heart. George Tuff's sons Jabez and Tom of Wesleyville, shared memories of their father which enriched and expanded the narrative. Bernice Clements and her brother Ken Mouland of Bonavista, niece and nephew of survivor Elias Mouland, also provided insight and detail, as did Thomas Dawson's niece, Theresa Dawson, Bay Roberts. Roland and Ina Abbot of Musgrave Harbour remember the old ways and stories, and like the others, passed them on with great kindness and generosity of spirit.

# PREFACE

Impossibility is at the centre of *The Harps of God*'s story. In 1914, for two days and two nights, one hundred and thirty-two sealers were lost on the ice fields of Newfoundland. No one knew they were lost. Captain Wes Kean, of the sealing party's home ship, the *Newfoundland*, thought the sealing party was on the *Stephano*, captained by the admiral of the sealing fleet, Captain Abram Kean. Captain Kean thought they were on his son's ship, the *Newfoundland*. The wireless radio of the *Newfoundland* had been removed to save costs, prior to this trip, by its merchant owners. An absurd combination of negligence, greed, incompetence and simple human error led to this dangerous and tragic scenario. Night fell and then the weather came. The first night, the sealers were caught in a snow storm that obscured their path back to their ship. That storm turned to rain and the drenched men were then subjected to a polar blizzard. Many men died. The next morning, the weather was sunny and clear. The survivors were within sight, even walking distance, of the many sealing vessels working the icefields. A barrel man on one of the ships spotted them and thought they were "this quare patch of seals lyin' around on the ice." No one knew they were lost and freezing to death on the icefields. The hypothermic survivors attempted to make their way to the ships. A heavy wind blew the men across the ice. The previous night's rain had caused a unique condition on the ice: fresh rainwater frozen on salt ice produces a particularly sheer surface. They had no footing and no strength. More men died. Another night on the ice and more men died. When so many died, how did one third, so few, survive?

Kent Stetson's *The Harps of God* poses the question, what does it take to survive? How does an individual find the will to survive in a hopeless and absurd scenario? Beliefs that the men relied on to survive in their isolated fishing villages are put to the test on the desolate icefield under a curtain of cold. In the end, their prejudices, their doubts, their bleak individual histories, their familial conflicts, their entrenched loyalties, and their myopic beliefs are what destroy many of the men's will to survive. Those who are angry, hateful, vengeful, and hopeless lose the courage or strength to survive. What they think will protect and save them becomes the means to their death. But those who accept the impossible and develop a particular urge to defy it; those who have a cultivated personal vision, an inclusive moral system, an understanding of contradiction, an ability to love, and a compassion for humanity; those are Stetson's survivors. The men's ordeal challenges their history and their very humanity.

The opportunity to direct *The Harps of God* at Rising Tide Theatre brought me to Newfoundland for the first time. Like, I suspect, most of us "from away," I wondered how these people survive, and how they did survive. Of course, how they do it struck me as just short of a miracle. One of the first things that Donna Butt, Rising Tide's Artistic Director, said to me was that the *The Harps of God* echoes the notion of Newfoundland as a "culture of tragedy." The play began to read to me as a microcosm of Newfoundland history. As the story moves through the two nights' and two days' ordeal, the society's divisions surface: schisms between Catholics and Protestants, Coakerites and merchants, conservatives and radicals are used by the men to justify the terrible choices they make in the name of survival. But in my research, I also discovered that England had never intended to colonize Newfoundland, and even created laws to prevent fishermen from settling there: it was too bleak, too unsustainable, and too uninhabitable. The fishermen who jumped ship and settled Newfoundland began life here by defying common sense, law, and order. Having done so, that first winter after the fishing fleet departed for England, they must have called upon a will to survive that would have brought every aspect of their humanity to a test. They survived.

On opening day of this play, it was raining in the morning. The premiere production was staged outdoors among the ruined foundations of a whaling factory. The factory was built on a precipice overlooking a beach below. This performance site is located in the middle of the bush across the harbour from the town of Trinity a ten-minute boat ride but a half-hour drive from the closest shelter. We were supposed to do our first and final dress rehearsal of the play in the afternoon. It was raining. I walked into the costume room as the actors were donning their costumes. For the first time, I saw them in their historically accurate costumes. What the sealers wore was so spare, such little protection—peaked caps with no protection for the ears; old soot-stained suit-coats with rope-belts for ties or just wool sweaters; leather boots that would easily become sodden with water; thin mitts and scarves. Hunting seals was such hard work that they dressed lightly, to prevent from overheating, sweating too much, and then getting very cold next to the skin. How little clothing they had to survive a blizzard.

How little clothing for actors to be wearing on a cold and rainy day. I told the actors they didn't have to do the dress rehearsal and we could easily cancel opening night. If the weather broke, we would just do our dress rehearsal that afternoon or night. The actors wanted to go on despite the weather. We joked that this was akin to the story itself. I said, "Yes but this is a play. You're actors, not sealers, and you don't have to put yourselves into harmful conditions."

Well, the cast brushed past me, defiant and determined, but not without humour. We loaded into our vehicles, drove to the site and did the first dress rehearsal. The rain stopped for most of it. Opening night, just before Act One commenced, it began to rain again. I told the actors they would have to project their voices according to the course of the rain. Through the first two acts of the play, it spat, it drizzled, and it fogged in. In the third act, it poured continuously. It was wet and cold for actors and audience. Our three-act play performed without intermission was already something of a marathon; the weather made it an ordeal. I expected the audience to abandon us any moment. But they stayed and the actors played on through the weather.

It was a riveting, intensely appreciated, and slightly miraculous opening night. What I saw that afternoon and that opening night, especially from the actors but also from the audience, was the courage and determination to go on. That defiance and will was at the heart of this group of actors from the Rising Tide Theatre, Trinity, Newfoundland. That defiance and will is at the heart of this play.

Richard Rose
January 10, 2001

# INTRODUCTION

Newfoundland is a "nation." We are a country with our own heritage, culture and sense of place. To Newfoundlanders culture is the blending of politics, economics and history into the human condition. Culture is the force that defines our country and our people, in essence a sense of identity. To understand *The Harps Of God* and its meaning to Newfoundlanders you must understand these essential truths. In Newfoundland and Labrador the past and the present lie side by side.

There are a few terrible great disasters that every Newfoundlander and Labradorian feels deep in their soul. These tragedies are of epic proportion, brought on by greed, power, arrogance and a reckless disregard for human life. They are burned into our hearts and stamped forever on our psyche as a people and as a "nation." The sealing disaster of 1914 is one such tragedy. It ranks with four others in our history:

The Battle of Beaumont Hamel, where an entire generation of young Newfoundland men were wiped out on July 1st, 1916. They were slaughtered by the enemy but callously sacrificed by the mother country. No regiment suffered more casualties than the Newfoundland Regiment. Every town and outport in the colony felt the loss and I am certain that for a variety of reasons Beaumont Hamel led to the suspension of our democratic government in 1933. As a child growing up, July 1st was not Canada Day, it was the day the best and the brightest of a generation were taken from us.

The resettlement program of the 1960s where thousands were driven from their homes by a federal/provincial plan to destroy the inshore fishery and drastically reduce our outport communities. This time a fiercely independent generation sacrificed, to make way for the glories and handouts of Confederation with Canada.

The loss of the Ocean Ranger, the giant oil rig that toppled into the sea on Valentine's Day, twenty years ago, killing 84 people on board. An unforgivable travesty.

And finally the cod moratorium of 1991, that brought to an end a once great fishery. This time an entire way of life was sacrificed forever.

These are not merely brief moments in history. They lie at the very core of Newfoundland's being. We are a strong, resourceful, resilient and stubborn people. We have suffered unbearable hardships with pride and dignity and an irrepressible sense of humour. The Newfoundland spirit is a powerful force indeed. And therein lies our great strength and our great weakness. We embrace disaster as part of our culture. This does not mean we wear death as some badge of honour, or that we welcome the grim reaper as our curse. But it does mean that our ability to endure and our faithfulness in remembering those who have gone before us has sometimes driven out rebellion and revolt. We endure, we struggle, we survive. Perhaps endurance is a badge of honour, a passage into nationhood.

The disaster of 1914 was not simply a force of nature. The elements were cruel and harsh as they often are out here in the middle of the Atlantic, but this disaster was man made. There were villains. A simple wireless removed to save a few dollars could have saved the lives of those men.

Kent's play of course, is about much more than merchants and power. I know that, and everyone who reads or sees this wonderful play will know that. The play encompasses the politics and the people. It is both intellectual and instinctive. Through the men on the ice we discover how unnecessary it all was. At the same time, we feel their personal agony. As Kent brings these characters to us, we see them not as frozen figures or political forces but as sons and brothers, husbands and boyfriends, fathers and uncles. We travel with Billy Pear as he returns to his mother's home, we watch Mamie joyfully dancing with her husband, and we imagine Arthur Mouland kissing his sweetheart one more time. Their struggle becomes ours as they fight to live. They come to us in all their flawed humanity.

But they are also forces. Tom Dawson believes men must not endure injustice, they must fight it. George Tuff knows no other way. For him, without the merchants and the great sealing captains, society would not be. He is an honest labourer, a toiler of the land and sea. In Levi, Kent has delivered up the old Newfoundland. A world where God was supreme and all good things came from above. A world of cold isolation and absolutes. A world where you honoured your father, your mother and your god, worked hard, and died. There was no other way for Levi. In Arthur Mouland Kent gives us the most complex of them all. With him we find redemption and hope. In the end he is guided by honour and duty but sustained by love. For me he bestrides two worlds. My political self stays with Tom Dawson on that ice but my gentler self occasionally drifts to Mouland, and finally my whole self soars with Kent's beautiful writing to that place where we dare to meet death and find peace.

Richard Rose talked about the opening night on the bare and barren ruins of the whaling factory. I remember holding an old umbrella over the stage managers script as the rain poured down on all of us so she could call her cues. It was an extraordinary night where for a few brief moments the men on the stage and the men on the ice seemed as one. The artist, the audience, the "nation," all for a moment up there on the edge of the world on those frozen ice floes daring the raging blizzard and crying out to whatever gods there be. Kent transported us there. In that moment I found myself embracing tragedy, honouring strength, and screaming at injustice. I came to think that perhaps it is through our disasters that we find our voice. It is said that in 1914 over 10,000 Newfoundlanders waited on the St. John's waterfront in solemn silence for the *Bellaventure* to return from the seal hunt with her grim cargo of bodies frozen forever in time. It is my fervent hope that we will continue to find voices that will break that silence. *The Harps Of God* helps us speak.

Kent's words captivated our hearts. We embrace him, and we salute our "Nation."

Donna Butt
Artistic and Executive Director
Rising Tide Theatre

*The Harps of God* was first produced by Rising Tide Theatre (Artistic Director, Donna Butt), Trinity Bay, Newfoundland, in August 1997 with the following cast:

Directed by Richard Rose

| | |
|---|---|
| George Tuff | Rod Miller |
| Arthur Mouland | Rick Boland |
| Tom Dawson | Melvin Barnes |
| Levi Templeman | John Ryan |
| Jessop Templeman | Peter Romkey |
| Simon Templeman | Dennis Hookey |
| Andrew Templeman | David Keating |
| Billy Pear | Michael Clarke |
| Lemuel Collins | Mark Critch |
| Richard McCarthy | Ed Kielly |
| Ambrose Mullowney | Paddy Monaghan |
| Willard Jordan | Douglas Ballett |
| Abram Kean | Reg Durdle |
| Peter Lamb | Chris Adams |

Deck Hands, Stewards, Barrel Man, Common Sealers, etc.
Peter Lodge, Dave Jerrett, Sheldon Cullimore, Luke Fisher,
Calvin Powell, Nicholas Bailey.

Set designed by Frank LaPointe
Stage managed by Lisa Millar
Assistant stage manager: Darlene Hollett
Costumes designed by Peggy Hogan
Props by Steven Locke
Production crew: Jim Pippy & Cory Jones

## CHARACTERS

| | |
|---|---|
| George Tuff, early thirties | Second Hand, *SS Newfoundland*. |
| Arthur Mouland, thirty-five | Master Watch, *SS Newfoundland*. |
| Tom Dawson, thirty | Master Watch, *SS Newfoundland*. |
| Levi Templeman, fifty | Common Sealer, *SS Newfoundland*. |
| Jessop Templeman, nineteen | |
| Simon Templeman, eighteen | |
| Andrew Templeman, sixteen | His sons. Common Sealers, *SS Newfoundland*. |
| Billy Pear, fifteen | Common Sealer, *SS Newfoundland*. |
| Lemuel Collins, twenty-two | Common Sealer, *SS Newfoundland*. |
| Richard McCarthy, thirty-nine | Common Sealer, *SS Newfoundland*. |
| Ambrose Mullowney, forty-two | Common Sealer, *SS Newfoundland*. |
| Willard Jordan, fifty | Common Sealer, *SS Newfoundland*. |
| Peter Lamb, twenty | Common Sealer, *SS Newfoundland*. |
| Abram Kean, mid-fifties | Master of the *Stephano*, Admiral of the Fleet. |

Deck Hands, Stewards, Barrel Man, Common Sealers, etc.

## SETTING

The North Atlantic; The front. Pan and slob ice, at the edge of the standing ice, forty two miles south-east of the Funk Islands; 48:12 N, 52:20 W.

## TIME

March 31, April 1 and 2, 1914.

## ACT ONE

*Ice grinds, cracks, and groans. A ship's engine fades.*

### MULLOWNEY

What a' ye make 'er, Dickey boy?

### MCCARTHY

I makes her any time she'll let me.
(*checks watch*)
Twelve ten.

### TUFF

Thomas. Lead the men south west.

### DAWSON

Me? You're the Second Hand.

### TUFF

I am that. Do as I asks and await further orders.

### DAWSON

From who?

### TUFF

From me.

### MULLOWNEY

This is a damn queer state of affairs.

### MCCARTHY

We takes our orders from the Master Watches out here.

### MOULAND

In the absence of the Captain, on vessel or on ice,
The Second Hand's always in charge.
Then 'tis the Master Watches.

### DAWSON

Not what I'd call a glittery day, George.

### TUFF

What?

### DAWSON

It's snowin'.

**TUFF**

I sees that.

**DAWSON**

Ye got your snow glasses on, b'y.

*DAWSON exits. The others follow.*

**MOULAND**

What'll we do about Bungay and Jones?

**TUFF**

(*pockets his dark, round snow glasses*)
Was it their men turned back?

**MOULAND**

Mostly.

**TUFF**

How many each?

**MOULAND**

Upwards of a dozen.

**TUFF**

I told Captain Wes 'twas too soon to make Master Watches of them.
Ye're able to read and write?

**MOULAND**

I am.

**TUFF**

If we goes soft on that slindgin' lot of hangashores,
'Twill knock things higher than a kite.
Find out their names and mark them down for me.
Captain Kean'll do the rest of it.
What do ye make of Dawson?

**MOULAND**

Tom's the strongest man on the ice.

**TUFF**

He's full of hard talk and black looks.

**MOULAND**

I'm more concerned about the Templemans.

**TUFF**

Levi Templeman's a saint.

**MOULAND**

The air's some thick between him and young Jessop.

**TUFF**

Levi can handle them boys.

**MOULAND**

Jessop was one of them that turned back.

**TUFF**

Jasus. All the more reason to keep our noses where they belongs–

**MOULAND**

I guess we're all a bit twitchy.

**TUFF**

–which is out of family business.

**MOULAND**

We got a pent up crowd of swillers eager to get among the fat.

**TUFF**

Somethin's chewin' at Dawson.
I believe 'tis me.

**MOULAND**

Word has it you got Tom's job.

**TUFF**

Second Hand, Master Watch or common sealer, 'tis all the same to me.
Two weeks stuck in the ice on that damned old tub.
I was like every other fella aboard of the *Newfoundland*,
Just itchin' to put on me seal skin boots.
Gettin' back among the fat, me son.
That's what matters.

**MOULAND**

Yes George, b'y. Nudding better.

**TUFF**

I was the happiest man in Christendom this mornin'
When Captain Wes ordered us acrost the ice to his fadder on the *Stephano*;
I swears I can smell d' swiles, Art b'y.

**MOULAND**

Things'll even out once the men is where they wants to be.

**TUFF**

There's no need to mark down young Templeman.

**MOULAND**

You're the boss.

**TUFF**

Let's go get everything wit' hair onto it.

*They exit. Cows call their pups; pups answer.*

**ANDREW**

Why do they call it a seal *hunt?*
They just lies there like a lump,
Wit' them big black eyes, and hollers.

**LEVI**

The Old Man hunts down the main patch, my son,
In hundreds of square miles of pack oice.
(*clubs a pup*)
It takes a keen mind knowin' current, wind and rafter–
And the ways of seals – to find 'em.

*Another seal pup calls, evoking the cry of a human infant.*

**BILLY**

Mewlin' and sobbin' for their mam like a little lost child.
(*imitates the whitecoat*)
And their mothers cries back;
It's a pitiable cry they makes–
Listen...

*A cow calls her pup. It responds.*

**ANDREW**

They're so purely white in appearance.
And so harmless, what?

**SIMON**

Ask a cod fish 'ow 'armless a swile is.

**BILLY**

Does swiles have feelings, do ye think?

**SIMON**

No, b'y. They're fish.
Fish don't 'ave feelings.

**ANDREW**

Fish? They're neither fish.
Look at them big black eyes.
Them is not the eyes of a fish.

**BILLY**

They're more the eyes of dog than fish.

**SIMON**

Well they're not the dog, me son.
(*clubs pup*)
They're a fish.

**BILLY**

Then why do they call them pups?

**SIMON**

They swims like a fish.
They're slick like a fish.

**ANDREW**

They tastes like a fish too.
Only worse.

**SIMON**

Ye 're that stun, Billy.
Why do ye think they calls it the seal *fish*ery if they're not *fish*?

**BILLY**

Same reason they calls them pups when they ain't dogs, I 'spose.

**LEVI**

For a clean kill,
(*club*)
Ye needs a smart blow to the top of the 'ead.

**SIMON**

(*club*)
I prefers a good smack to the snout.

**LEVI**

Eider way...
(*sculping*)
Whatever gits the best job done wit' the least amount of effort;
Ye've a long day of fat before ye, so pace yerselfs.
Watch now, Andrew.
Roll 'e over and slit 'is belly from asshole to appetite.
Draw yer blade forwards in one clean cut...

**DAWSON**

Mind what Skipper Levi says, Billy.
Yer turn's coming.

**LEVI**

Through the hide and fat, neither deep nor shallow.
Mind you don't nick the sack that holds the guts.

**DAWSON**

Take yer knife, Billy, and cut around one front f'ipper.
Leave the other attached to the pelt;
Ye takes them home to yer mother.

**SIMON**

A salt barrel of f'ippers'll keep 'uns family well into the fall.

**LEVI**

Leave the 'inder daddles onto the carcass.

**ANDREW**

Seems a shame to leave so much behind.

**LEVI**

We've no use for them.
Mother nature's a tidy creature, not prone to waste.

**MCCARTHY**

There's no sight dearer to a cod then a ripe morsel 'a seal guts
Waftin' down to 'e when the ice thaws.
Makes him feel there's some kind of justice after all.

**MULLOWNEY**

(*club*)
Although ye never knows the mind of a fish.

**DAWSON**

Muck around in the fat now, Billy,
And give them skinny whoppers a good greasin';
Work it into the uppers, right up to the knees.

**BILLY**

Yes sir, Skipper Tom.

**ANDREW**

Here, father; Mr. Swile and his skin is parted for good.

**LEVI**

Well done, me son.
We'll make a proper swiler outa' ye yet.

**BILLY**

Mother says, even after ye removes it from his body,
A young swile's skin stays in secret sympathy wit' the sea.
Years later, when the tide ebbs in the full of the moon,
The hide... ruffles.

**SIMON**

That's just woman's talk.

**JORDAN**

(*sculps*)
One thing you'll learn when your time comes, b'ys;
Woman's talk best be heeded.

**MULLOWNEY**

We all knows who's in charge of Newfoundland.

**MCCARTHY**

That's right, me son.
'Tis neider ye nor I nor the King of England.
(*club*)
'Tis the missus.

**LEVI**

Make two small slits just above the h'eye.
Pass your 'aul rope t'rough.

**DAWSON**

Here ye go Billy.
(*club*)
I'll kill em, you sculp 'en, till ye gets the hang of it.

**BILLY**

Them big black eyes lookin at me.
What am I to think?

**MULLOWNEY**

I thinks of me youngsters
All decked out in new shoes and coats.
Then *Whammo!*
(*club*)
One less seal, that many more cod fish,
The youngsters turned out proper;
The pride of Pouch Cove.

**MCCARTHY**

(*club*)
The merchant off of me back for half an hour.

**DAWSON**

Think of yer old retriever, Billy,
The day we put him out of his misery.
What a wonderful relief it was to the lot of us.

**BILLY**

Includin' the dog?

**MULLOWNEY**

I thinks of Mamie's big pink thighs,
On a blowy Saturday night.

**LEVI**

There's no call for yer dirty Irish smut, Mullowney.

**MULLOWNEY**

Mind yer business, you arse-clenched Protestant kill-joy.
Mamie and me dancin' and dancin' and...
Oh, Jesus boys.
(*club*)
I miss me Mamie somethin' fierce.

**DAWSON**

Hop to it, Billy.
(*club*)
Ye're one behind already.

**LEVI**

Captain Kean says this year'll provide the biggest bill ever,
Despite the late start.

**JORDAN**

Another Eldorado spring.

**SIMON**

Rumours of war in Europe 'ave sent the price of seal oil skyrocketin'.

**ANDREW**

There's all kinds of uses for the fat–

**SIMON**

Oil for the soldiers guns–

**ANDREW**

Oil for the machines that'll stitch their uniforms.

**JORDAN**

Fine light oil, seal oil.

#### MCCARTHY
What soldiers?

#### ANDREW
We're goin' to make our fortune, Billy.

#### MULLOWNEY
There's talk of war in Europe; where ye been, b'y?

#### MCCARTHY
Home, me son.
(*club*)
Mindin' me own business.

#### JORDAN
Them boys of yer's 'ave got right knowin'.

#### LEVI
I took 'em to The Nickel in St. John's town.

#### JORDAN
The things youngsters learns at them damn movin' pictures.

#### LEVI
(*club*)
Shockin'.

#### BILLY
Where's their harps to?

#### ANDREW
It's only the growed up cows and dogs got the harp.
Eh, father?

#### LEVI
That's right, me son.
And why's that, do ye suppose?

#### ANDREW
(*sculping*)
When God hurled Lucifer into the abysmal deep,
There was a great racket and row in heaven.
God's favourite possession–
A little harp, made of solid gold,
Wit' the sweetest voice ever heard–
Was knocked off of her cloud and plummeted into the ocean.

#### LEVI

God was fit to be tied.
(*club*)
Why? Simon!

#### SIMON

First he's forced to throw Our Saviour's big brother Satan out of 'eaven.
Then he loses his most cherished possession.

#### LEVI

Satan was the older brother of God, not Jesus.
God was about to loose his mighty vengeance upon the earth...
What 'appened? Andrew!

#### ANDREW

He heard the sweetest of sounds.
Yes, sir. He did. Down north – off of the Labrador–
Glintin' like a miracle above the tempest tossed sea...
There she was, b'ys;
The little gold 'arp of God.

#### BILLY

No!

#### LEVI

Yes. Simon!

#### SIMON

Yes father.
A young dog seal – a beater, not yet a bedlamer,
Just after losin' his white coat and takin' to the water–
Seen the glitterin' object waft downwards to the floor of the sea.
Now, seals is a wonderful playful creature, as we all knows.
That's why they gets so tangled in our nets,
Rippin' and tearin', causin' no end of labour.
Ruinin' our hard work.
(*club*)
Damn their hides.

#### LEVI

Bless their 'ides fer the life they gives, says I. Andrew!

#### ANDREW

This young seal seen there was somethin' particular about the golden 'arp.
Not only did she hum the loveliest tune,
But she spoke to the young beater and said–

**BILLY**

No, Skipper Levi b'y! She never! She spoke?

**LEVI**

Oh, yes my son. She said...
"Take me home to me fadder, and 'e will reward ye."
Well sir. He took her in his mouth,
Swam to the surface and danced in the wind and foamin' waves,
Balancin' God's 'arp on his nose, safe among the starm.
The wind caused her strings to quiver, then 'um–
Then, Oh...!
That mournful song.
My son.
God was that pleased.
You know what he done?
(*club*)
He took back his harp and said to the beater – Simon!

**SIMON**

Yes, father.
God says to the young swile:
"Thank you, my son.
As a sign of my pleasure, you will bear the shape of my 'arp on yer back.
Yer children will sing her mournful song.
For yer supper, I'll make the seas team wit' fishes like nowhere else on earth.
I'll cause ye and yer tribe to swell in yer multitudes 'till the end of time."

*Art MOULAND enters. JESSOP Templeman follows.*

**LEVI**

Andrew!

**ANDREW**

The beater said "Thank ye, heavenly father."
For as we knows, swiles could talk back then–

**MCCARTHY**

That's right.
(*club*)
And tight-arsed moralizin' old Protestants wasn't invented yet.

**ANDREW**

"But we am perfectly happy the way we is,"
Says he, and swum away.

**LEVI**

God was beside himself wit' rage:
"Why you uppity little bag of fat and guts.

(*club*)
Thinks your perfect, does ye?
I'll have none of that."
God was that angry. Why? Simon!

### MOULAND

Go ahead Jessop.

### JESSOP

Father, I come to say–

### LEVI

Simon.

### JESSOP

I come to say I'm sor–

### LEVI

Simon!

### SIMON

Because from the moment of creation until then,
The souls of all God's creatures—men, seals, fish, everyt'ing—
Was in perfect 'armony wit' his own.
Perfect as the sounds from the 'arp of God.

### LEVI

That's right.
Every thing and every body knowed their place in the scheme of things.
God in 'eaven at the top, the lowest worm on the bottom;
Mankind in between.
And God gave man dominion over everyt'ing that walked,
Squawked, crawled on its belly, flew in the air or swum in the sea.

### MCCARTHY

Then, for some damn reason,
(*club*)
He invented merchants.

### LEVI

That trouble wit' Lucifer broke out.
All hands started singin' their own tune.
We all knows where that leads to.
God called him back.
"In yer arrogance you deny me;
From this day forward, you will offer your very skins
And those of your children,
To the sons of men for their benefit;

(*club*)
At my pleasure." Andrew!

### ANDREW

Yes, father. Mr Swile dove, rose up
Broke the surface wit' a wonderful flip, and said:
"They'll have to catch me first."

### LEVI

So God took the swile's arrogant, willful voice from him;
Made 'im croak like a frog; bark like a dog.
Then 'e hobbled the disobedient creature's youngsters.
Made them creep about on the oice on their bellies,
(*club*)
Easy pickin's
For the great ice bear and the sons of men.

### MULLOWNEY

Fairy stories.
Sure, the truth of the matter is we'm hungry and them is food.
Food and clothes for me.
(*club*)
And my Mamie.

### DAWSON

And yer dear mother. For you too, Billy.

### JESSOP

There was sun hounds, Father;
Clear as I ever seen them.
Two little rainbows, one on eider side,
In the ring around the sun–

### LEVI

"Behold, the hand that betrayeth me is wit' me."
What's he doin' 'ere?

### JESSOP

I thought it was orders.

### LEVI

You was lookin' for the easy way out.

### SIMON

As usual.

### JESSOP

Everybody knows sun hounds is a sign for weather.

**LEVI**

I seen no sun 'ounds.

**JESSOP**

Skipper Alpheus John Harris seen them.
So did the others.
Skipper said, "It looks for weather for certain.
If I have a few more men wit' me,
I'll head back to the *Newfoundland*."

**LEVI**

All I seen was a Templeman on a long 'ard march,
Turning his back on his brothers and his father.
Alright Jessop.
You're among the real men now,
Not luxuriating aboard of the *Newfoundland* wit' them desertin' sleeveens;
There's a whitecoat fer ya.
Club 'e.

**JESSOP**

I can't.

**LEVI**

Don't you go soft on me.

**JESSOP**

It turns me guts.

**LEVI**

'Tinks yer better'n the rest of we do ye?
By God, King Edward and Captain Abram Kean,
Ye bloody well *will* do it.

**JESSOP**

No, sir. That's what I will not.

**LEVI**

Defyin' yer father in front of the men. Who do ye think ye is?

**JESSOP**

I was following orders.

**LEVI**

Here's yer orders, boy.
Kill swiles like the rest of us.

**JESSOP**

Ye can't make me.

#### LEVI

That's what I can and that's what I will.

#### JESSOP

(*raises gaff, horizontal*)
No.

#### LEVI

(*grabs gaff*)
What's wrong wit' ye?

#### JESSOP

I can't tell the difference between meself and the swile pups no more.

> *LEVI lands a glancing blow to JESSOP's jaw. JESSOP stands, unmoving.*
> *LEVI moves to strike again. In self defense, JESSOP straight-arms his*
> *father. LEVI stumbles, falls to the ice. JESSOP moves to help. SIMON*
> *levels JESSOP, with a blow to his face. JESSOP sprawls; hand to nose –*
> *blood. SIMON helps his father stand. MOULAND hands JESSOP to his*
> *feet.*

#### MOULAND

Get back to yer watch, Jessop.
Go on now. *Go!*

> *JESSOP exits.*

#### DAWSON

We ain't got forever, Billy.

#### ANDREW

All right, b'ys... here goes nothin'.

#### BILLY

Me too.

#### DAWSON

Good lads.

#### LEVI

Yer mothers'll be proud of ye.

#### ANDREW

(*clubs pup*)
Augh! Father!

#### LEVI

Don't ye go turnin' coward on me too.

**ANDREW**

That felt–

**LEVI**

Never mind 'ow it felt.

**ANDREW**

–good.

**DAWSON**

Billy. Ye're next.
A good stout blow, now–

*BILLY raises his gaff. A strong gust of wind. Blinding snow.*

**LEVI**

Lord Jesus.

**BILLY**

Skipper Tom!

**DAWSON**

Stay where ye're to 'till she clears.

*The wind drops. The squall clears. TUFF enters.*

**TUFF**

Come on boys.
Finish up and move three pans to the west.

*TUFF exits.*

**MULLOWNEY**

What time do ye make 'er, Richard?

**MCCARTHY**

I find the morning's best, when she's rested.
She's pushin' three.

*MCCARTHY exits followed by JORDAN and the rest of the men.*

**LEVI**

Damned Irish smut.
(*straightens, pain*)
Me poor old bones is full a' weather today.
"Wind from the east, bodes ill for man and beast."

**MOULAND**

Maybe he's not cut out for the swillin' game, Levi.

**LEVI**

I would'a passed 'm me gaff and stayed to 'ome wit' the missus.
But young Andrew 'ad me drove near cracked.
'E needed to learn, 'tis my job to teach him.

**MOULAND**

I meant Jessop.

**LEVI**

I once heard Abram Kean say to your father,
"Fine swilin' crowd, you Moulands.
I wish 'twas all Moulands."
Ye should take pride in that, Art.
I know who ye meant.

**MOULAND**

Simon and Andrew are great young swilers–

**LEVI**

"Happy is he who departs this world wit' a good name."
You know what it is to get a berth to the front.
And you knows the way the Captain Kean t'inks, well as I do.
If Abram hears my Jessop turned back at the first sign of 'ardship,
That'll be it for the Templemans.
We can't live without the seal fishery anymore than you can.
Willful young devil.
Hadn't been for Simon, I believe I woulda' killed him.

**MOULAND**

We all loses our way betimes, Levi.

**LEVI**

Last four years, that young fella reaped a bloody whirlwind of fat and 'ides.
Killed more than men twice his age.
I made sure Captain Abram Kean knew of it.
I said to his mother,
"Now there's a young fella fit to take me place.
The Templemans'll 'ave berths wit' Captain Kean long as our Jessop's alive."
He defied me; in front of the men.
He knocked me down.

**MOULAND**

He was protecting himself–

**LEVI**

He might as well took a gun and shot me.

**MOULAND**

Many a good men is better off ashore.

**LEVI**

They ain't Templemans.
How do ye know what my Jessop is or isn't?

**MOULAND**

I knows what I sees before me.

**LEVI**

'Tis a dreadful thing to sire a willful child.
I believe he was born wicked. God forgive me, I do.

**MOULAND**

I've yet to see a child born evil, Levi.
I believe it's us that twists them out of shape.

**LEVI**

Come back when ye're a man wit' grown children.
We'll talk of the 'ard 'arted fathers of ungrateful sons then.

*LEVI exits. DAWSON enters. They pile sculps.*

**DAWSON**

Blessed is the peace makers.

**MOULAND**

What makes good men like Levi Templeman turn so 'ard?

**DAWSON**

I does what I does to survive.
I allows Levi do the same thing.

**MOULAND**

I learned to bend wit' the wind.
Otherwise I'd 'a snapped long ago.

**DAWSON**

Care for a snort, Art?

**MOULAND**

No, b'y.

**DAWSON**

Nothin' puts lead in a fella's pencil like Radway's Ready Relief.

**MOULAND**

Now there's a slogan, if I ever I heard one.

**DAWSON**

I can see it in the *St. John's Daily Mail*,
Right next to the society column.
Radway's Ready Relief served at Government House;
His Excellency's missus was heard to say,
"That'll put lead in yer pencil, Gov b'y."
Are ye sure?

**MOULAND**

Yes, thanks all the same.

**DAWSON**

Ye're purer than God hisself these days.

**MOULAND**

Did ye ever fall in a hole so deep,
Neither light nor dark could penetrate?

**DAWSON**

Not that I can recall.

**MOULAND**

Well, I did.
Did ye get that wire out to yer father?

**DAWSON**

No, I never. Old man Kean said,
"The *Stephano's* wireless is for business only,
Not a toy for common sealers."

**MOULAND**

Captain Wes woulda' let you use the *Newfoundland's*.

**DAWSON**

Yes, I allows Wes would. If he had one.
I never seen a son so unlike 'is father,
As Wesley Kean is unlike that old bastard.

**MOULAND**

He's a kind hearted young fella.
Too kind for the swilin' game, some says.

### DAWSON

God help us.
You shoulda' seen me own poor old father.
Too sick to stand.
White as a ghost.
Spittin' blood.
First year home, away from the hunt, since he was fourteen.
"Wire me when ye gets to the front, Thomas b'y.
Let me know when you're among the fat."
Captain Wes took me to the wireless room.
There's nothin' left but danglin' wire.

### MOULAND

The talk goin' around is,
The Harveys refused to lay out the five dollars to hire an operator.

### DAWSON

How many ships in The Harvey's Fleet?
How many men here on the ice, at their mercy?
How much money does that bloated crowd of blood suckers need?

### MOULAND

It always come down to one thing with them fellas.

### DAWSON

We're no more than dogs to them.
They'll beat the life right out of us,
Until we stands up on our own hind legs and says, "No more."
It's a new age dawnin', Art b'y;
Prosperity for all, arising from equality–
No more masters and servants.
All for one, my son. And one for all!
That's the future.
We're part of it.

### MOULAND

Says who?

### DAWSON

William Coaker; The Fisherman's Protective Union.
Men out around the bay, in every town and harbour:
Up along, in Canada; Halifax, Winnipeg, Vancouver,
Down in Chicago, New York, The Boston States.
All acrosst Europe.
Men are standin' up for their selves, sayin':
"You and me will advance for who we are
And what we got to offer."
No more kowtowing to the likes of Abram Kean,
And that damn greedy pack 'a jackals he runs wit'.

Seal oil and salt fish will belong to them as gathers it.
We'll sell all over the world, direct to the highest bidder.

### MOULAND

I always said there's way too much up top
And too damn little down below.
It's ignorance and poverty that rules out around the bay.

### DAWSON

That's the way the merchants likes to keep it.
The people got no kind of life at all.

### MOULAND

How many more got to die of this damn scourge,
Coughin' up their life's blood like your poor father?

### DAWSON

There's more to existence than bare bones survival.

### MOULAND

Truer words, b'y–

### TUFF

(*off*)
Mouland!

### DAWSON

We'll stand eye to eye wit' Old Man Kean and his ass kissin' lackeys.
We'll pay our own way wit' the best of them.
We'll be men, not beasts of burden.

### MOULAND

Sounds good to me.
I'll take a piece of that.

> *MOULAND exits. DAWSON's men copy on—i.e., vault with gaffs from ice pan to ice pan—over open water. TUFF follows.*

### DAWSON

Come on, me sons.
I hears a patch 'a fat off to the west,
And time's marchin' on.

### LEVI

'Tis now or never, Billy.

### JORDAN

Come on me son. Ye can make her.

> *BILLY vaults, loses his footing. Willard JORDAN grabs him. BILLY Pear*
> *falls backward, dragging JORDAN into the water with him. JORDAN*
> *brings BILLY to the surface by the scruff of the neck.*

**DAWSON**

Billy!

**TUFF**

Tom. Gaff Willard. I'll get the lad.

**DAWSON**

The boy's my responsibility.

**TUFF**

Do as ye're told, Dawson.

> *BILLY and JORDAN are gaffed, dragged onto the pan. BILLY lies*
> *motionless. JORDAN crawls away.*

**DAWSON**

Billy. Billy!

**TUFF**

Lie him on his back. Willard! Someone grab a holt a' Willard.

**DAWSON**

Sit up. He's not breathin'. Sit up.

**TUFF**

He's took on water.

**ANDREW**

Billy.

**DAWSON**

Billy. Breathe, b'y. He ain't breathin'.

**TUFF**

Find his breast bone. Press... easy! Ye'll crack it.

> *Stillness... a cough then BILLY's blind, flailing panic. ANDREW*
> *restrains him.*

**BILLY**

Mother? I'm all wet mam.

**ANDREW**

Billy. I ain't yer mam.
I'm Andrew Templeman from Little Catalina.

**Billy Pear Comforted.**

*(l to r)*
Dennis Hookey,
John Ryan,
Michael Clarke,
Melvin Barnes,
*(background)*
David Keating,
Ed Kielly.

**TUFF**

Come on, boys. Keep them from the wind.

**JORDAN**

Oh, Jesus.

**DAWSON**

Circle round. Who's got any Radway's?

**MCCARTHY**

(*offers flask*)
I do.

**TUFF**

Willard. Willard! Ye fell in the water.
Do ye hear me?

**JORDAN**

Oh, Jesus.

**TUFF**

I knows, b'y, I knows. Take a swally.

**JORDAN**

God help me.

**TUFF**

Come on b'y. 'Tis Radway's Ready Relief.

**MULLOWNEY**

Sure, it's good for what ails ye.

**MCCARTHY**

Yes b'y, and if nothin' ails ye
It's good for that too.

**TUFF**

Hurry, now, so I can get some into the young fella.

**DAWSON**

Billy. Heave a glutch of Radway's into ye.

**BILLY**

(*he does, spews it*)
It's got alcohol into it.

**MULLOWNEY**

Only twenty-five percent.

**MCCARTHY**

Don't go wastin' it.

**BILLY**

I promised me mother
I'd never touch liquor as long as I live.

**MULLOWNEY**

How'll he get thru' life wit'out a drop of Radway's?

**MCCARTHY**

You never knows the mind of a Protestant, sure.

**TUFF**

Our best bet is the ship. Get up and movin' men.

**JORDAN**

Leave me be.

**BILLY**

Skipper, ye saved me life.
Come on, now. Up ye gets.

**DAWSON**

That's the way, b'ys. All for one, now. And one for all.

**JORDAN**

Bless yer heart, Billy... ye're a good lad.

**TUFF**

Tom, go find Art Mouland.
Tell him not to let his men stray too far afield.
Bring him here.
Then find Jones and Bungay–

**DAWSON**

These here is my men.
My job, as I understands it, is to look out for them.

**TUFF**

Do ye know me favourite story?
It's about the good shepherd who went in search of the lamb that went astray.
He left the ninety and nine–

**DAWSON**

We're not sheep.
And despite there's three feet of oice below yer feet, Tuff,
Ye're a long ways from walkin' on water.
Round them up yerself.

**TUFF**

Thomas, listen.
I got a hundred and thirty men scattered all over hell's half acre.
I got two wet men and there's weather on.
I'm lookin' at the strongest man on the ice,
A man the good lord made a leader, not a follower.

**LEVI**

Do as he asks, Tom.

**DAWSON**

Keep an eye on Billy, here, will ye Levi?
Do what Skipper Levi tells ye 'till I gets back, now, Billy.

*DAWSON exits.*

**LEVI**

C'mer, Billy.
Yer a h'onorary Templeman 'till Tom gits back.

**JORDAN**

I needs a bite 'a grub.

**MCCARTHY**

Yes, b'y. Old Man Kean was awful damn close wit' the food bag.

**MULLOWNEY**

Fifteen minutes aboard the *Stephano*–

**MCCARTHY**

After a six hour march over five miles of shiftin', rafted ice–

**MULLOWNEY**

Weak tea and one damn maggoty biscuit per man;
The very soul of generosity.

**TUFF**

The Admiral had his own crew to feed.

**LEVI**

We could all use a mug up.

**TUFF**

All right. Five minutes. Shelter the wet fellas.

**MULLOWNEY**

Whata' ye make her, Dickey b'y?

**MCCARTHY**

(*watch*)
I makes her toes curl and her eyes roll back in her head.

**LEVI**

There's no call for smut.

**MCCARTHY**

Smut's like beauty... in the mind of the beholder.
Not yet four o'clock.

*They dig out food bags. BILLY gnaws at a piece of bread.*

**ANDREW**

Billy, ye're makin' precious little 'eadway, gnawin' at that excursion bread.

**BILLY**

There's nei'der tea to soften it.

**MCCARTHY**

Here. Ye needs a good dose of rolled oats and raisins.
Chip a bowl outa the ice and mix them up wit' some water.

**BILLY**

Maybe I'll slosh a dollop of Radway's into it.

**MCCARTHY**

That's the spirit, Billy me son.

**BILLY**

Don't nobody tell me mother.

**TUFF**

I'm sure she'd understand, under the circumstances.

**BILLY**

No, Skipper. That's what she would not.
Ye never know'd me father.

**TUFF**

Was any of yez ever out wit' Skipper Billy Winsor?

**MCCARTHY**

Yes, boy. His first year Skipperin' the SS *Beothic*.

**LEVI**

Now there is a great man.

**TUFF**

Skipper Billy? I loves that man.

**MCCARTHY**

He's a jowler, true enough.

**JORDAN**

Finest kind.

**MCCARTHY**

Shockin' fond of a chaw, Skipper Billy.

**LEVI**

Yes, my son. Great talker.
Loves his chew of twist, too.

**MULLOWNEY**

Sleeps on his face, they says,
To keep the 'baccy juice from runnin' down his throat.

**MCCARTHY**

Is that so?
That'd explain the yellow beard.

**MULLOWNEY**

Yeah.

**TUFF**

This one time, we'd panned a good few seals and it got right airsome.
Skipper Billy couldn't find us.
So he got on the *Marconi* toot-sweet, fired off a message to the *Florizel*.
Of course she was away and gone already.
So there we was.
It black as pitch.
Us uns stuck.

**MULLOWNEY**

Well, b'ys... there's five.
Let's get back to the ship.

**MCCARTHY**

That's never five minutes, Mullowney.

**MULLOWNEY**

I don't sleep all that well on ice.

**MCCARTHY**

Calm yerself.

**LEVI**

A night on the oice'll put hair on a fella's chest.
If it comes to that. Eh Billy?

**BILLY**

Yes sir. S'pose.

**JORDAN**

(*trembles*)
Sure, a man don't feel himself a proper sealer
Less he's been on speakin' terms wit' death a time or two.

**TUFF**

Anyway, night come thumpin' down hard and fast,
Like she does on the oice in a starm.
Never mind that, we says.
We'm alright.
We cut up our tarred and fatty tow ropes,
Frizzed them out to start a fire.
We had thirty seal carcasses and the fat of the sculps.
Kept it fair roaring, like a furnace.
Gave us all the roasted meat we could ask for too.
Well sir. Around midnight,
Every man went and got himself a live young seal.
And that's what we sat on.
There we was, squat on our fat little thrones smokin' our pipes,
Huddled up agin' the storm.

**MCCARTHY**

Squirmy little fat thrones, no doubt.

**TUFF**

No sir. The height of comfort.

**LEVI**

They don't seem to mind.

**TUFF**

They never shifted. Not a biver.
Sure, every once in a while they'd open their eyes, look around.
Then go back to sleep, content for the company.

**MCCARTHY**

They're built to stand tremendous pressure, ye know.

**TUFF**

Oh my yes. By morning, they was black as soot from the smoke.
Like the rest of us.

**MCCARTHY**

Except where yer arse ends was to.

**MULLOWNEY**

They didn't bear the mark of the harp of God that mornin'.

**MCCARTHY**

No, boy.

**MULLOWNEY**

No.

**TUFF**

No.

**MULLOWNEY**

Well... I hears a plate of hot beans wit my name on it callin out, "Eat me, Ambrose."

**JORDAN**

Man dear, it was hell on earth.
First time I ever seen the beast.

**MULLOWNEY**

Jesus H. Not another friggin' yarn.

**MCCARTHY**

Listen and learn, b'y. A good tale saved many a man's life.

**BILLY**

W'as the beast?

**ANDREW**

A creature wit' long sharp horns–

**LEVI**

There's no such animal.

**JORDAN**

Indeed there is; what do ye think the bible's about?
And you a man forever quotin' chapter and verse.

**TUFF**

The beast is mankind's worst fear.
'E feeds on human cruelty and weakness.
'E lives deep inside each and every one of we.

**JORDAN**

There's times he comes out of his hole in the pit of yer stomach,
Stands before ye.

**TUFF**

All of a sudden out of the drift was the loom of somethin' immense.
I kept me head and stared at it hard as I could.
It was gone quick as it come.
I shudders just to think on it.

**MULLOWNEY**

It's a damned fib, the beast.
Dreamt up by some Protestant crack-pot from Pouch Cove,
To scare innocent children.

**BILLY**

Like a bull, or what?

**TUFF**

An oice bear. A bull. A man.

**JORDAN**

All three. 'Tis made of fire and ice.

**LEVI**

Pagan nonsense.

**JORDAN**

I never seen Jesus Christ or the Virgin Mary out on the oice.
But I sure as hell seen the beast.
The old folks says the red-moon beast wit' two horns blazin'
Means the loss of a great many lives.

**TUFF**

Not the night I'm speakin' of, it never.
I'll never forget me first glimpse of the *SS Beothic* that morning.
I was away from the crowd on the small ice come the dawn.
I can't think why.
The snow was that heavy it lay thick on the water.
'Twas a job to tell it from good ice;
One false step and...
The sight that met me eyes sends shivers through me still;
Outa the drift, bow and scuppers festooned wit' icicles of blood, appeared–

**BILLY**

The beast!

**TUFF**

Ha! No b'y. The *Beothic*!
They'd loaded bloody sculps all through the starm, see.
So she ended up with this blood red beard 'a oicecles... musta weighed a ton.
Imagine that comin' at ye full tilt outa nowhere.

**LEVI**

There's yer beast, Jordan.
There's a reasonable explanation for everythin'.

**JORDAN**

Maybe so. Maybe not.

**TUFF**

I knows one thing.
Skipper Billy Winsor was right heedful where he dropped his men after that.

**MULLOWNEY**

Unlike Abram Kean.

**TUFF**

From that night forward,
We was wonderful heedful to stay handy to our ship.

**MCCARTHY**

Live and learn.

**MULLOWNEY**

You'd like to think so.

**MCCARTHY**

I suppose 'twas them seals that saved ye.

**TUFF**

Yes, b'y. In a queer way, I s'pose t'was.
Tide and time waits for no man.
Let's get up and movin' b'ys–

*Howling wind.*

Lord God. Brace yerselfs.

**ANDREW**

Father!

**LEVI**

Andrew, me son!
Stay where ye're to.
Where're ye at, Simon?

**SIMON**

Here, father. Wit' Skipper George.

**TUFF**

Levi. Have a t'ought fer Willard Jordan.

**JORDAN**

I'm the finest kind.

**MULLOWNEY**

McCarthy?! Richard?

**MCCARTHY**

Here, Ambrose.

**LEVI**

Andrew me son. Where's Billy?

**ANDREW**

Here, father. Wit' me.

**TUFF**

She's lettin' up. Let's travel, b'ys.

**BILLY**

Me specs keeps clumpin' up wit' this wet snow...
The more I rubs them clear, the worse they gets.

**LEVI**

Andrew, pull young Billy along wit' ye.

**BILLY**

Yes, Andrew. You be me eyes.

**ANDREW**

Alright. Hang on.

**BILLY**

That's it. Ha! Fast as any other man on the ice.

**MULLOWNEY**

Where are we goin' to spend the night, George b'y?
The *Stephano* or the *Newfoundland*?

**JORDAN**

The *Stephano*'s comin' back for us, that's what I heard.

**ANDREW**

I say we makes back for the *Stephano* now.

**LEVI**

This is business for the men, Andrew.

**ANDREW**

I killed me first seals. Amn't I a proper man now?

**LEVI**

Yes, b'y. I suppose ye is.

**ANDREW**

All right then. I say we makes back for the *Stephano*.

**TUFF**

We'll head to the *Newfoundland*.

*DAWSON enters.*

**MULLOWNEY**

You can march us five miles
Over shiftin' ice in man murderin' weather before dark?

**TUFF**

We're closer to the *Newfoundland* by half.

**DAWSON**

Which way, George?

**TUFF**

'Tis a warmish wind out of the southeast. Keep it on yer left cheek.

**MCCARTHY**

The wind is shiftin', George, b'y. Ye'll have us walkin' in circles.

**DAWSON**

Lay down yer compass and give us a bearin'.

**TUFF**

Clean up this patch of white coats then head south by south east.

**LEVI**

B'ys, we better do as he says.

**MULLOWNEY**

No.

**JORDAN**

No.

#### MCCARTHY

No.

#### DAWSON

Which way, George?

#### TUFF

Lay down yer compass. Plot a course south by south east.

#### DAWSON

The man in charge lays the course.

#### LEVI

Give us a reading, George.

> *They wait.*

#### TUFF

I can't.

#### MCCARTHY

What do ye mean ye can't?

#### TUFF

I mean I can't.
I left me compass aboard of the *Stephano*.

#### MULLOWNEY

Jesus, Mary and Joseph.

#### MCCARTHY

Forty miles from the nearest land wit' no compass.
In March. In a snow storm. In shifting ice.

> *DAWSON produces his compass, lays a course.*

#### TUFF

What did I ever do to ye, Tom?

#### DAWSON

Yer head's full of Protestant shepherds and Catholic sheep.
You and Old Man Kean, b'y?
Ye're the wolf at my door.

#### TUFF

Catholic or Protestant's got nothin' to do wit' it.

#### MCCARTHY

And hogs don't like slop, do they George?

*The wind gusts. A cow calls for her pup. Ice cracks and grinds.*

#### COLLINS

(*off*)
Skipper George.

#### TUFF

Who's calling?

#### COLLINS

Lemuel Collins, Sir.
(*enters*)
I found the path we cut this mornin' on our march to the *Stephano*.
It's marked clear by blood from sculps
Alpheus John Harris and them drug back to the *Newfoundland*.

#### JORDAN

Likely leads right back to the ship.

#### MCCARTHY

Them hangashores might'a saved us a night on the oice.

*MOULAND enters.*

#### MOULAND

I say we all collects back into our own watches.
Four columns of forty men each movin' parallel
Will travel faster than one long shaggy line.

#### TUFF

Make it three columns, not four;
Combine Jones' and Bungay's watches, put them in the middle.
It'll be easier to keep track of their men.
Tom. I wants you at the head of that centre column.
You're the man wit' the compass. You'll lead.

#### DAWSON

All right.

#### TUFF

Arthur. Send Jones and Bungay to the tail end of yer and Tom's columns.
I'll lead from the rear, keep an eye on them and watch out for stragglers.

#### MOULAND

Good. I'll put Cecil Squires at the head of yer column.

#### TUFF

Simon.

**SIMON**

Yes sir?

**TUFF**

Find Jones and Bungay and tell them what's what.

**SIMON**

Done.

*SIMON exits.*

**MOULAND**

I'll keep my boys to the east of Tom.

**DAWSON**

Keep in shoutin' distance of each other.

**TUFF**

Good. Sing out every five minutes or so;
I wants to know the whereabouts of every man on the ice,
Every step of the way.

*Exit MOULAND and DAWSON.*

**TUFF**

Lemuel. Take five or six of the smartest men ye can find.
Go like the wind to the ship.
Don't let up 'till ye're aboard of her; tell Captain Wes to lay on that whistle
Till' he see's each and every one of our boot-ugly faces.

**COLLINS**

Yes sir.

**TUFF**

Lemuel?

**COLLINS**

Sir?

**TUFF**

Put wings on them feet.

**COLLINS**

Aye Skipper.

*Exit COLLINS.*

**TUFF**

All right, me sons. We're going home.

*A ship's whistle. They stop.*

The *Stephano*?

#### LEVI

Yes, b'y.

#### MCCARTHY

Not far to the rear.
Just passin' through, no doubt.
Likely pickin' up our pelts, claimin' them for the *Stephano*.

#### MULLOWNEY

Thievin' old scoundrel.

#### TUFF

There's no turnin' back now.

#### LEVI

No me son. And no need to either.
Our ship's to hand.

*TUFF exits.*

#### MCCARTHY

I swear to God I can smell the *Newfoundland*.

#### MULLOWNEY

Does she smell any better than when we left her?

#### MCCARTHY

No b'y. Still ripe as a bucket of tripe in August.

#### MULLOWNEY

All them years of seal and whale fat gone rancid.

#### MCCARTHY

She'd make a goat lose his dinner.

*The* Newfoundland's *whistle, nearby.*

#### MCCARTHY

The *Newfoundland*, ahead.

#### MULLOWNEY

Simon never got there that quick.

*A second blast. They wait. Wind.*

### MCCARTHY

Why in the name of God would Captain Wes give two blasts then quit?

### LEVI

I allows twasn't for us.
Likely had fellas out cuttin' ice or dumpin' cinders.

### MCCARTHY

The first sounded due south.
The second sou' east. I wonders how far?

### LEVI

Hard to say wit' the wind.
No more than two or three mile.

### MULLOWNEY

What time's it now?

### MCCARTHY

Damn near dark is what time it is.
There's not a half hour 'a light left.

*Lightning. Thunder. Enter SIMON.*

### SIMON

The blood trail leads to the edge of the next big rafter.
The pan past it wheeled ninety degrees in the wind.
Beyond that, there's nothin' but a jumble of new snow and slob ice.
The trail's lost.

*Pouring rain. The men stand motionless. The rain ceases gradually.*

### MULLOWNEY

Jasus. I couldn't be wetter if I'd took a dip.

### MCCARTHY

Nout but a warm shower, outa the south.

### LEVI

Pray to God it stays sou'ward, and recommences rainin'.
If she backs to nor'ard and comes on cold...
God help us.

*TUFF copies on, followed by COLLINS.*

### TUFF

Now boys. It looks like a night on the ice.
All we have to do is put up wit' it like little men.

**COLLINS**

Art Mouland got his crowd buildin' gazes out of chunks of ice.
Each gaze'll have its own fire, and shelter ten or so men.

**TUFF**

Set to work on a gaze here.

*The men gather trim and stack chunks of ice.*

Lem. Get Jones and Bungay goin' on theirs.

*Exit COLLINS.*

**BILLY**

Have ye ever seen the beast, Andrew?

**ANDREW**

No, b'y. But Jessop did.

**SIMON**

Pinwheel eyes squirtin' blood.
Feet like the great white ice bear–

**ANDREW**

'Cepts, where it walks, flames sprouts.
Terrible big claws. Long horns keen as a gaff spike.
Great jaws slobberin' the worst kind 'a p'ison.

**SIMON**

The face of a man, lips all blackened, chawed off by oice and frost.
The most wonderful kind of fangs.

**ANDREW**

It's a coward, see.
If ye looks away, he grabs ye quick as a wink.
He hugs ya right close–

**SIMON**

It stinks somethin' wicked–

**ANDREW**

Then it eats the head right off 'a ya.

**SIMON**

Sometimes it just nips ye.
They say folks once bit longs for death.
Ye becomes a beast yerself see.
Ye craves the taste of human flesh evermore.
The beast was once a human like ye or me–

**BILLY**

What'd he do?

**SIMON**

Jessop? He stared it right in the eye, like ye're s'posed to.

**ANDREW**

'E blowed away in a swirl of hair and fur, for 'e has both.

**BILLY**

Jessop?

**SIMON**

No, b'y. The beast.

**LEVI**

Simon. Stop that profane jibber.

**SIMON**

Yes, sir.
(*quiet*)
Andrew? I t'inks Jessop got nipped.
In the struggle.

*Sudden wash of light.*

**TUFF**

She's damn near full, but still waxing.
Tomorrow night, I'd say, she'll be full.

**JORDAN**

Take and put yer left hand before ye... like this... d'as it.
The old folks says the wanin' crescent is the left horn of the beast.
Means times past. Life's decline. The end of things.
Fits snug into the curve of yer left hand, look. Like a sickle.
Now the right... like this.
The crescent moon waxin' is the beast's right horn.

**TUFF**

The new moon's a brand new boat, me sons,
Sailin' empty across the sky.
Nothin' in her hull, full of promise nonetheless.

**SIMON**

The virgin, waitin' to be filled.

**JORDAN**

Put yer finger and thumb of ei'der hand together... da's it.
There she is. Herself. The full moon.

**TUFF**

The white full moon is a ship makin' harbour,
Her holds full to bursting, her decks awash with plenty.

**LEVI**

In times of turmoil, the blood red moon hangs low on the horizon.

**JORDAN**

The beast afoot wit' two horn's blazin'.

**SIMON**

Father? I wants to find Jessop.

**LEVI**

Leave him bide by hisself 'til he's ready to do 'is duty.

**SIMON**

I promised Mudder I'd look out for 'im.

**ANDREW**

Father? He belongs here. Among family.

*DAWSON copies on.*

**SIMON**

Skipper Tom? Where's our Jessop to?

**DAWSON**

Wit Jones and Bungay two rafters north east.
Be awful careful. The winds swingin' nor'ard.
The pans is loose and shiftin'.

**SIMON**

Father?

**LEVI**

Keep yer eye on them clouds.

*SIMON exits. BILLY is lost in high-speed, repetitive motion.*

**LEVI**

Thomas. Young Billy's lookin' wonderful ragged.

**DAWSON**

Billy, come here and set a spell.

**BILLY**

What?

**DAWSON**

Andrew. Take a holt of young Billy and slow him down.

**TUFF**

Willard. Willard, b'y? Bless yer heart ye're barely movin'.

**JORDAN**

Tall as three men. Terrible stink. Its eyes is blood, George.
Its breath is flame. Its heart is solid ice.

**TUFF**

Come here and set. Leave yer jacket on.

**JORDAN**

(*steps out of trousers, removes jacket*)
I'm goin' to bed.

**TUFF**

No. Ye ain't no such thing. Put that back on.
(*helps JORDAN dress*}
Let's ye and me have a bit of a scoff.
On the menu is sardines, oatmeal and a glutch of Radway's.

**JORDAN**

Just a swally. I'm that dry... thanks, George b'y.
Don't tell the men I'm feelin' low.

**TUFF**

No.

**JORDAN**

And don't mind Tom Dawson.
There's not a better man on the ice when it comes down to it,
Unless it's ye yerself.
A kinder man never walked than ye, George Tuff...
They'll have great need of kindness now. And a firm hand.
George boy. I'm that hot...

**TUFF**

We're takin' a little stroll, Willard.

*A small pan of ice. Variable moonlight. SIMON copies on.*

**JESSOP**

What do ye want, little brother?

**SIMON**

Ye should be wit' us.

**JESSOP**

Did he send ye?

**SIMON**

No.

**JESSOP**

Then I'm where I belongs.

**SIMON**

We're buildin' a gaze, then we're goin' to light a fire.

**JESSOP**

Christ, Simon. I coulda handled another punch from him.

**SIMON**

Ye struck our father.

**JESSOP**

I held him back, that's all.

**SIMON**

Ye knocked him to the ice.

**JESSOP**

He tripped. Ye seen me. I offered our father me hand.
As far as I was concerned it was over.
Ye broke me nose.

**SIMON**

I'm sorry.

**JESSOP**

Are ya? I don't think ye is.
Ye're right where ye always wanted to be.
At the head of the line for that fine gold watch of his.

**SIMON**

Go to hell.

**JESSOP**

I'd say we're there already.

**SIMON**

Ye're gone soft.

**JESSOP**

I lost me taste for blood.
Who's the better sealers now, Simon?

Head-bowin' fools, soaked to the skin, like to freeze to death?
Or the men who read the weather right and had the good sense to turn back?
Ask him that for me, Simon. That'll drive'm into the fits.

### SIMON

Come ask him yerself.

### JESSOP

Why would I? I already knows 'is answer.

### SIMON

Coward!

*High wind. Sudden cold.*

### JESSOP

You damned sook. Get back to the old devil before you loses yer place in line.

*SIMON exits.*

### TUFF

She's swung around nor'ard, down from the Labrador.

### JORDAN

Cold boys. She's comin' in awful cold.

### MULLOWNEY

Oh, Jesus.

### LEVI

Get to the edge of the pan and sing out to yer brother in a good loud voice.
Don't stop until ye sees 'is face.

### ANDREW

Simon!

### MULLOWNEY

We built ourselves a wall of ice. Now we're pinned against it.

### ANDREW

Simon!

### MULLOWNEY

(*walks the perimeter*)
There's nothin' behind it but water. Christ on the cross.
A night 'a high wind and snow... right smack in the gob.

**MCCARTHY**

We'll each have a shell of ice when this freezes.

**ANDREW**

Simon!

*SIMON copies on.*

**SIMON**

Quit yer bawlin'.

**ANDREW**

Did ye find Jessop?

**LEVI**

Never mind Jessop, now. Look out for yer own skins, my sons.

*MOULAND copies on.*

**MOULAND**

All hell's broke loose on Jones' and Bungay's rafter.
Can ye take ten or so Tom?

**DAWSON**

Of course.

**TUFF**

Is there a rafter of any size close to hand?

**SIMON**

For all of us? No, b'y.

**LEVI**

Have a care, Thomas. Ye got yer own forty, and these wet fellas to look after.

*JESSOP copies on.*

**LEVI**

Get back to yer watch.

**JESSOP**

I don't want to be alone.

**LEVI**

None of yer damn tricks.

**JESSOP**

I'm sorry.

**LEVI**

Tell it to yer friend the devil.

**JESSOP**

I just did, didn't I?

**LEVI**

Get out of my sight.

*A blast of wind. JESSOP exits.*

**JORDAN**

Cold.

**MULLOWNEY**

Perishin' cold.

**MCCARTHY**

Cold as a merchant's heart.

**JORDAN**

Look! God have mercy. Look!

**TUFF**

What?

**JORDAN**

Terrible jaws. And blood.
Oh! The eyes. The terrible eyes!
The stink. The terrible smotherin' stink.
We're all gonna perish. Each and every one, b'ys.
Old and young alike.

*Willard JORDAN sinks to the ice, lies on his side. TUFF struggles to rouse him. JORDAN dies.*

**TUFF**

Willard? Willard! Jesus b'ys.
Willard Jordan kept me goin' through the worst night of me life.
Now look at him, poor soul.

**LEVI**

Prepare yerselfs, men.

**MULLOWNEY**

He's right. We're all gonna smother. We're all gonna perish.

**ANDREW**

I ain't allowed to perish, Skipper.
I promised me mam; I'm goin' home.

**LEVI**

Das it, my son."The Lord is my shepherd– "

**BILLY**

I good as killed Skipper Willard Jordan.

**DAWSON**

It wasn't you got us lost, Billy.

**TUFF**

Ye've been hard against me all day. I wants to know why.

**DAWSON**

Captain Wes said "If it looks for weather, stay aboard the *Stephano* wit' me father."

**TUFF**

He never.

**DAWSON**

He did. Before half of us gets Old Man Kean's weak tea and hard tack into us,
He's herdin' us off the *Stephano*, in a snow storm,
Tuff here bowin' and scrapin',
Tellin' him it looks for weather, the old bastard quotin' the barometer,
Which has been stuck on fair since Harveys installed the damn thing, sayin',
"It doesn't show for weather, George me son,"
Despite what he see's before him.
Then he says, "Go clean up that patch of fat and make for the ship."
Ye said "Which ship?" He said "The *Newfoundland*."
He did George b'y. I swear to God b'ys, he did.
And it, five mile away, stuck in the ice with weather comin' on.
The *Stephano* cuts through the ice like butter, b'ys.
Coulda come back an' got us in half a minute.
Ye never batted an eye, did ye?

**TUFF**

Ye're promotin' mutiny.

**DAWSON**

Do ye want us all dead?
Or is yer head so far up that Old Man's arse
Ye're startin' to see the world through his eyes?

**MOULAND**

Tom. That'll do.

#### DAWSON
First ye steals my job, then ye commandeers me men.

#### TUFF
It was never yer job.

#### DAWSON
I was next in line.
Too bad I was the wrong race and religion.

#### TUFF
That's a damn lie.

#### MCCARTHY
English Protestant lordin' it over Irish Catholic;
Tis a truth old as Newfoundland.

#### TUFF
I was the better man.

#### DAWSON
Prove it.

#### TUFF
Any time, any place.

#### MOULAND
George–

#### DAWSON
Right here, right now–

#### MOULAND
Stow it. Grow up for Christ's sake the pair of ye.
The men look up to you, Dawson.
Tuff, the job at hand is to survive this night
And lead these men back to the *Newfoundland*.

#### TUFF
Poor Will Jordan... what'm I to tell his missus?

#### MOULAND
Never mind that now. The men is countin' on you, George.

#### TUFF
What if me strength fails?

**MOULAND**

I'll lend mine. If mine fails, I'll look to ye.
And to you, Tom Dawson. And to Levi Templeman here.
We'll get through this night by countin' on each other.
What do ye say, Tom?
What is it... all for one and one for all?

**DAWSON**

All right.

**MOULAND**

George?

**TUFF**

The *Newfoundland*'s our best hope.
First light, we're makin' for her.

**MOULAND**

Good. Get these b'ys to work on a new gaze.

> As MOULAND copies off, moonlight fades. TUFF drags JORDAN's body
> to shelter.

**BILLY**

I killed Skipper Willard.

**DAWSON**

Willard Jordan could'a left ye bide in the water.
He didn't, did he?

**BILLY**

No sir.

**DAWSON**

He struggled to save ye of his own free will.
That made him a better man and ye a lad wit' a tale to tell.
Let's ye and me talk about other things 'till ye warms up.

**BILLY**

Yes sir. Skipper Tom? Does the beast ever go ashore?

**DAWSON**

Why do ye ask?

**BILLY**

Me mother.

**DAWSON**

The beast lives in the minds of poor, ignorant souls like Tuff and Jordan.
Yer dear mother's safe as churches.
Come on, me son.

*Moonlight fades. Thick snow. Heavy wind.*

**DAWSON**

Let's get the men to work on a new shelter.
One that's got two sides to it.
What was they thinkin', building it on the edge.
We'll be spinning around like a top all night;
Pitchin' and yawin' like a ship at sea.
We'll all hang on fer dear life and have a dandy ride!
That'll be fun, eh Billy me son?

**BILLY**

Yessir, Skipper Tom.
'Spose.

## ACT TWO

*Night. Wind. JESSOP, on an isolated pan, supports a young sealer.*

### JESSOP

Henry? Name of God. Henry?
(*lowers Henry's body to the ice, rises*)
Is anyone there?
(*hunched against the cold*)
Someone.
Help!
(gust of *wind*)
Run. No. Just wait. For what?
Run like the wind and don't stop 'till ye gets...
Where? Anywhere.
Henry... Henry?
Damn ye to hell for a coward Henry Dowden.

> *Art MOULAND enters, comes to the edge of the water that separates him
> from the pan on which JESSOP scavenges Henry's belongings – jersey,
> sculping knife, etc.*

### MOULAND

Jessop? Who's that?

### JESSOP

Henry Dowden.

### MOULAND

He was a friend of yours.
Leave the dead lie in peace, b'y.

### JESSOP

Him and me was boys together.
Not a day went by we never seen each other.
He was more brother to me then me own two brothers.
Never done a tap 'a harm to no one.
Henry was my friend.
Why poor Henry?
Why not me?

### MOULAND

There's no answer to that question.
None that will satisfy.
Where's Jones and Bungay?

**JESSOP**

They forced us onto this little pan.
Took our haul ropes to burn, and our gaff handles.
They're like a pack of hungry wolves.
Or somethin' up out of the grave;
Losin' their minds. Turnin' on each other.
Me and Henry was gettin' far from this cursed rock as we could.
Wine women and song, b'ys.
Halifax. Montreal. The Boston States.

**MOULAND**

I had the same notions once.
Turns out everything I needed to know, I learned at home.

**JESSOP**

I knows all I needs to know about Newfoundland.

**MOULAND**

One night in St John's town a poor fool went drinkin' wit' the devil.
Seemed a nice enough fella.
Only the devil had a knife.
The poor fool found himself face down in an alley.
People took one look and passed him by.
A young woman recognized the poor fool–
Someone from back home, he was–
Layin' there moanin' in his own blood and vomit.
She set him up, looked into his eyes; she said his name.
Death hightailed it in the opposite direction.

**JESSOP**

The fool in the alley was ye.

**MOULAND**

My Belle tended me wounds and saved me life.
I hates to see another human bein' suffer so.

**JESSOP**

Who says I'm sufferin'?

**MOULAND**

Look at ye... pacin' forward and back like a caged animal.
Come back wit' me, Jessop.

**JESSOP**

Good Saint Art, is it? Ye'll save yer own pelt.

**MOULAND**

I will. And as many else I can.
My "pelt" don't belong to me alone now;

My Belle is waitin' for me ashore.
She's got the most precious thing on earth growin' in her belly.

### JESSOP

Another simpleton born to work his guts out,
To keep some miserable old son of a bitch merchant in the fat.

### MOULAND

You got a mind of yer own and yer old man hates ye for it.
Am I right?
Mine drowned himself in fish guts and misery.
Then set about pullin' me under wit' him.
He was squat little bull of a man, like meself.
Fishermen, wha'?
We're bred compact fer hard work in tight quarters... so they says;
We takes up less room below decks, and if a fella goes overboard,
Solid muscle sinks quicker than flesh.
Yes, b'y. Hard hearted fathers. Ungrateful sons...
Long as I was a boy, things was dandy.
My best friend in the world, my old man;
'Till I come into me own manhood.
He's dead these fifteen years. I'm terrified of him yet.
I spent half the time angry at meself for bein' afraid.
The other half afraid of me own anger.
P'isoned wit' guilt.
And so damn sad.
I got away alright. Then set about creatin' me own misery,
Far worse than any the old brute ever handed out.
On the run, goin' nowhere.
Whorin', brawlin' – the promise of me young manhood
Streeled out behind me in a string of empty bottles.
My so-called friends liked me better drunk than sober.
They was the bars of a cage of me own makin'.
My Belle rattled the door, said,
"You kept it up some nice me son,
But whoever threw ye in here is long gone.
Look at this. They left the door wide open.
Come out my son. Have a look around."
Well, sir. I did.
I seen that lovely woman... my Belle;
The sea washin' through her,
Full 'a tides and currents,
Her heart awash with yearnin';
Mine like foam on the sea...
Love's the antidote, me son.

### JESSOP

All the love on earth can't keep a cold man from dyin'.

**MOULAND**

Can't it? I got the chance to start over.
Nothin' says you won't too.


**JESSOP**

Along comes friggin' Simon. Then Andrew.
The old man casts me aside and worships them.
'Specially friggin' Simon.
Miniature copy of himself.
All I heard from then on was,
"Look out for yer brother."
"Ye've had more than yer share."
"Grow up, for God's sake. Act like a man."
Act like him, he was sayin'.
Well, I'm not him. I'm meself.
Save yer talk of love for yer poor sap of a child, Mouland.
I heard it all before.
Who am I, he hates me so?


**MOULAND**

There's not much left in yer little fire, Jessop.
Join up wit' us.

**JESSOP**

I'd rather die here by meself then come up against Jones and Bungay and them.
Or that old bugger... 'tis all the same to me.

**MOULAND**

Things is orderly back at my gaze; every fella lookin' out for the other.
I haven't lost a single man, and that's how I intends to keep it.
Come wit' me. Ye'll be taken care of.

**JESSOP**

Is that a promise?

**MOULAND**

It is.

**JESSOP**

What odds? No future here.

> MOULAND *throws his gaff across to* JESSOP, *who prepares to copy from the opposite side of his pan into darkness.*

**MOULAND**

Are ye determined to die by yerself, in the black of night in a blizzard?

**JESSOP**

No Skipper. That's what I am not.
I got a gaff now.
What more do I need, besides sunrise?

**MOULAND**

You haven't got a gaff.
Ye've got my gaff.
Jessop! If ye gets back to the *Newfoundland*,
What'll ye say about the men ye left behind?

**JESSOP**

I'll tell them what I tells you.
I'll tell them me father sent me.

**MOULAND**

You steal me gaff, ye leave forty men wit' a crippled leader.

**JESSOP**

Thirty men left me and Henry to die.
Fair's fair.

**MOULAND**

Fair has nothin' to do wit' what ye intend.
It's easy, picking bad over good.
Yerself over others.

**JESSOP**

You got an opinion on everyt'ing, ain't ye?

**MOULAND**

It's the sum total of a man's choices that make his life, Jessop.
You've got a choice, here and now.
No less a choice than evil or good.
I answered yer call for help.
Please. Help me to help my men–

**JESSOP**

I seen somethin'... somethin' terrible.

**MOULAND**

What.

**JESSOP**

Henry.
I stood there, talkin' to him.
I seen him... he just slipped away.

**MOULAND**

'Tis hard to watch a man die;
'Tis far worse to feel yerself slippin' away.
If the devil'd finished me off that night in St. John's town,
I believe I'd 'a come back from the dead and thanked him.

**JESSOP**

For what?

**MOULAND**

For ending my misery.
The best life had to offer, stole out from under me, and I'd 'a thanked him!
Ye mustn't live yer life believin' yer stuck, that things don't change.
They do, my son, for better more often than worse.
I needs that gaff, Jessop b'y.
I'm their leader.
They depends on me.

**JESSOP**

That's where we differs.
I was taught to depend on no one but meself.
(*at Henry's body*)
Shag ya. Ye're not totally useless.
(*takes Henry's food bag*)
Ye won't be needin' this.
(*pulls scarf free*)
Or this.

> *JESSOP exits. The fire dies.*

**MOULAND**

Jessop! Jessop!!
(*in the darkness*)
God help us.

> *Exit MOULAND. The wind rises to great fury, diminishes, blows a steady gale. Still, silent figures shuffle to life.*

**MULLOWNEY**

(*breaks stance*)
Jenny? Take yer little brother by the hand, me maid,
And come away from that fire. Jenny!
Don't be teasin' yer poor father.
(*close to the edge*)
Jenny, maid... please. Come away, now.

**COLLINS**

Hold on there Skipper. You're walkin' in yer sleep.

**MULLOWNEY**

I'm wide awake. Is it still dark?

**TUFF**

Black as pitch.

**COLLINS**

Your eyes is all iced over. Skipper George.
Do ye know this man?

**TUFF**

No, boy. His face is all swolled up and purple.

**MULLOWNEY**

Mullowney. My name is Ambrose Mullowney.

**TUFF**

Get the ice off of him or he'll lose his sight for good.

**MULLOWNEY**

Lose me sight!?

**DAWSON**

The man can still hear.

**MULLOWNEY**

Me socks is froze to me pants. They're hard as a nut.
Me mitts and sleeves shrunk away in opposite directions.
Me wrists stopped burnin' hours ago.
I believes me ears has turned to solid ice.
Christ 'a mercy. I can't go blind too.

**COLLINS**

Skipper, I want ye to bend, can ye?
I got to chew the ice off of ye.

**MULLOWNEY**

(*bends to Collins*)
My eyes is wonderful cold.

**COLLINS**

(*chews at iced brows and lashes*)
I know, Skipper. Be still.

> *A second sealer panics, grabs Collins.*

Get him off of me.

**TUFF**

Calm down. Who are ye?

*The sealer roars.*

**DAWSON**

Easy now. Richard McCarthy, ain't ye?
Your moustache and beard's iced together.
Richard. Calm yerself.

**TUFF**

Get to work on McCarthy, Lem.
That ice builds up anymore, he's liable to smother.

**COLLINS**

There ye go, Ambrose.

**MULLOWNEY**

The ice is off?

**COLLINS**

Yes, b'y.

*MCCARTHY presents himself.*

Nothin' disgustin' lurkin' in that moustache, is there Skipper?

**MULLOWNEY**

Oh God. Everythin' is pitch black.
I'm blind!

**DAWSON**

Your eyes is wide open.

**MULLOWNEY**

I'm blind!

**TUFF**

You're not blind, b'y. It's night.
You're starin' into the dark.

**DAWSON**

Look to the light of the fire, Ambrose.
(*turns him*)
There.

**MULLOWNEY**

Thank God.

**MOULAND**

(*off*)

When we got home there was somebody there,
Somebody home we liked.
When we got home there was somebody there,
In the kitchen window a light.

**LEVI**

What's that foolishness?

**COLLINS**

Some recitation Art made up.

**MOULAND**

(*off*)

Alright now, everybody...

**SEALERS**

(*on the wind*)

When we got home there was somebody there...
Somebody home we...

*The wind rises; voices fade.*

**COLLINS**

Mouland's got his men stood up in rows, markin' time like soldiers.
Every man thumps the back of the fella in front.
The front man takes the brunt of the wind for a spell,
Then shifts back to the heat of the fire.
He hasn't lost a single man.

*DAWSON drags a corpse to shelter.*

**DAWSON**

When did the pelt of a seal take on more value
Than the life of a Newfoundland fisherman?

**MCCARTHY**

When did Christ last walk on water?

**LEVI**

Keep yer blasphemous smut to yourself.

**DAWSON**

You'll never see a merchant froze to the ice.

**MCCARTHY**

We puts food on their table, the likes of which we'll never taste.

**DAWSON**

Our sweat sends their sons and daughters
To the finest schools in London England and Paris France;
How many of our own can write their name or ever hope to read a book?

**MCCARTHY**

They owns us the day we're a-born;
As they owned our fathers before us.

**TUFF**

What makes either of ye any better?
William Coaker and that union crowd ye runs wit'?
So long as every fella thinks just like ye and don't step outa' line
'E's a great smart fella.
But woe be-the-tide the little man who thinks for hisself.

**DAWSON**

Think like a little man, a little man ye'll ever be.

**MCCARTHY**

A man who rules another owns a slave.

**LEVI**

You try running a fleet of sealin' vessels wit'out a strong right arm.

**MCCARTHY**

Bob Bartlett and Skipper Billy Winsor have their men's respect.
They earns it wit' a firm 'and, sure enough.
They looks out for their men like their own family.

**DAWSON**

Abram Kean treats fishermen like coin of the realm;
We comes and goes and that's our value.

**MCCARTHY**

'E treats them boys of his, Captain Wes and them, like they was little gods;
Us like we's his property... there's the difference.

**MULLOWNEY**

What time is it?

**MCCARTHY**

Me watch is in me pocket and me pocket's froze shut.

**MULLOWNEY**

Who the hell are ye? And what are ye doin' in my kitchen?
Jennie.
I wants ye up them stairs and fast asleep be the time yer mudder gets 'ome.

**MCCARTHY**

I'd rather slit me own throat than go like that.

**COLLINS**

What?

**MCCARTHY**

Mullowney. Crazy as a bag of hammers.

**COLLINS**

At least he ain't doin' no harm, poor soul.
Aside from settin' a bad example.

**DAWSON**

Give us yer gaff, now Billy.

**BILLY**

I can't.

**MULLOWNEY**

Mamie. You're home.

**DAWSON**

Sure ye can, me son. Ye got no need of it tonight.
Snap the head off of it, now, and throw the shaft on the fire,
Like the rest of us done.

**MCCARTHY**

Tis only an old stick, sure. The woods is full–

**BILLY**

You said a man's gaff is the difference between life and death on the ice.

**DAWSON**

None of us wants to die, Billy.
But none of us 'as got the right to keep for hisself what other fella's needs.

**BILLY**

But we'll be sealin' tomorrow.

**DAWSON**

I'll fix a new shaft onto it when we gets back to the ship.
C'mon, Billy. It's not like ye to be so pig 'eaded.

**BILLY**

I never even killed me first seal.

> BILLY *attempts to separate shaft and gaff head. Too weak, he gives it to*
> DAWSON.

**Mullowney,
Mad with Cold,
Hunger and Fear.**

*(l to r)*
Ed Kielly,
Paddy Monaghan,
Rod Miller.

**DAWSON**

T'row the shaft on the fire, now; and keep the head close by ye.

**SIMON**

That's it Billy.
Think of us comin' home, our pockets stuffed wit' dollar bills.

**ANDREW**

And a barrel of swile f'ippers on our backs.

**DAWSON**

Think of yer dear mother and the look of 'appiness on 'er face
When she sees ye alive and well.

**ANDREW**

Yes b'y. Yer brothers and sister dancin' around,
Singin' "It's our Billy, Mother. Our Billy's home from the swiles."
Oh my... what a hero ye'll be.

**SIMON**

The man of the family.

**BILLY**

What'll happen to me if ye...?

**DAWSON**

Who says I'm going anywhere?

**BILLY**

You can hardly walk.

**PETER**

(*enters*)
George b'y. Tom. Ye knows me.
I'm Peter Lamb from Shambler's Cove.
I can't feel me fingers.

**TUFF**

I can't help that, Peter.

**PETER**

Art Mouland drove us from 'is fire. We's perishin'.

**COLLINS**

I seen what ye crowd done.
They forced Art and them away from their own fire.

**PETER**

It's some 'ard to freeze in the dark;
Knowin' there's 'eat and grub not sixty yards away.

**TUFF**

Grub? There's no grub here.

**PETER**

They says they is. And gaff handles.
We wants to build some kind of fort or other, see?
Or build a tower, then set a beacon fire.
Or just burn them for the heat.

**TUFF**

We got nothing more.

**PETER**

You still got yer gaff.

**TUFF**

We needs at least the one to get to a ship.

**PETER**

Ei'der gaff 'andle, George b'y? Or a bit of rope?
I can't say what'll happen to me if I goes back there empty 'anded.
Even a spell at the fire. Just meself. Just a minute or two.
I's a thin little stick of a fella. I won't take much. Please...
I'm begging ye.

**TUFF**

If I gives in to one fella, well... ye knows the rest.

**DAWSON**

Peter, listen. We'll let each man take turn about,
Every fella gettin' a few minutes next the fire
Then allowin' another up close and so on.

**PETER**

Aye sir.

**DAWSON**

They'll do as I say. Will they? Peter?
I'm holding ye responsible.

**PETER**

Aye sir.

**SEALER**

Help us, won't ye Tom?

**DAWSON**

Alright. It's all for one and one for all boys.

**COLLINS**

I'm tellin' ye, ye'll regret it.

**DAWSON**

Hush, Lem. Alright. Pair off and come forward two at a time.

*Sealers push forward in a rush.*

**MULLOWNEY**

Get back ye damned greedy sons of bitches. Get back.

**PETER**

We got a right to food and warmth like any other man on the ice.

**DAWSON**

That's what I'm sayin, Peter. But only if we portion out our–

**SEALERS**

Cold. Perishin' cold...
Help us...
Just a bit of heat...

**TUFF**

Listen to me, every man jack of ye. There's a chain of command–

**SEALER**

Just a bit of heat, b'ys...
Just a bite of grub...

**TUFF**

I'm tellin' you. There's no grub left. There's no more rope or wood–

**PETER**

Tuff's lyin'. Look at 'is gaff. He's keepin' it fer hisself.

*MULLOWNEY gaffs a corpse, drags it toward the fire.*

**PETER**

Burn the dead.

**LEVI**

Yer chain of command is as chaff in the wind, George.

**MCCARTHY**

Stop, ye damn mad creature.

**PETER**

It's one for all, ain't it? Alright. One dead for all the livin'.

**DAWSON**

B'ys. Listen to me. Ye knew this man.
Some of ye knows poor Aldis' wife and child.

**TUFF**

If ye survive this night, and you do this awful thing,
Margaret will know what ye done to her husband.
Because I'll be there to tell her–

**PETER**

Tuff and Dawson's lookin' out for themselfs.

**DAWSON**

When have I ever broke my word? When?

**COLLINS**

Never is when.
Listen ye damn fools. Listen to Tom Dawson.

**DAWSON**

Men of the *Newfoundland*.
I'm telling' ye the truth. We have one chance–

**PETER**

Burn the dead.

**SEALERS**

Burn the dead!

**MCCARTHY**

The wolf's at the door, Tom b'y.
Ye don't negotiate wit' the wolf.

**TUFF**

I'm givin' ye an order, Dawson.
Control them men.

**DAWSON**

Order the wind to drop.
Order the sun to rise and warm these poor creatures wit' a ray of hope.
Order yer friend Abram Kean to appear through the storm
Wit' a hot kettle of tea and yer compass home.
(*moves to the fire*)
We'll get back to our families by lookin' out for each–

**PETER**

Lookin' out for yourselves!

**TUFF**

I am tellin' – orderin' every man to do what he can to stay alive.

**LEVI**

Orderin' a man to stay alive is like tellin' that fire to keep burnin'
When there's no more fuel.

**TUFF**

If ye got a better idea, let's hear it.

**PETER**

I smell burnin' flesh.

**DAWSON**

Peter. Step back from the fire.
Ye're frost bit, my son. Ye can't feel the heat.

**SEALERS**

Save us. Help us.

**PETER**

Damn liar. You're roastin' pork, and here I am starvin'.

**COLLINS**

Go on. Roast the flesh off yer damn greedy hands and face.
That's the way.
Roast and eat yer own cooked flesh.

**DAWSON**

Lemuel. Come away–

**COLLINS**

Take off yer coat. Throw it into the fire.

*PETER does.*

**COLLINS**

That's the way. Why stop there?
Throw yer whole ignern't self into it.

*PETER stumbles forward into the embers. DAWSON drags him to safety.*

**COLLINS**

In the name of God. I didn't mean it.
Skipper George? I didn't–

**Peter Lamb Seeks Heat Among the Ashes.**

*(l to r)*
*(on concrete set, stage right)*
Michael Clarke,
Mark Critch,
Rod Miller.
*(upper level)*
Ed Kielly,
Dennis Hookey,
David Keating,
John Ryan.
*(centre, concrete set)*
Melvin Barnes,
Chris Adams.
*(stage left)*
Peter Lodge,
Dave Jarrett,
Sheldon Gullimore,
Luke Fisher,
Calvin Powell,
Nicholas Bailey.

**TUFF**

Lemuel. It's not your fault.
Get a holt of yerself. Do ye hear me? Do ye?
Go get Art Mouland.

> COLLINS exits. MULLOWNEY claims the fire, defends it, his gaff
> a spear.

**MULLOWNEY**

Ah. Mamie. Ya knew I was comin' in cold and empty.
Grand fire, me love.
Ye built it up nice for me.
It's Saturday night, the rum is cold and the fire's hot;
The youngsters is upstairs, hard asleep.
Put on yer dancin' shoes, missus.
Me and you is goin' t' have ourselfs a time.
Sweet Jesus.
The curtains is burning.
The curtains is burning!

> MULLOWNEY destroys the fire. TUFF and DAWSON advance.
> MULLOWNEY holds them at bay with his gaff.

**MULLOWNEY**

Get back ye damned slinks of hell.
Touch my Mamie and I'll stick ye like the pigs ye are.
Mamie. Where were ye?
There ye are. The most beautiful woman on God's earth.
(*He waltzes among the ashes.*)
How lucky was I to catch yer eye?

**BILLY**

Mullowney was bit by the beast.

**DAWSON**

Come away Billy.

**TUFF**

The sun's not an hour away.
Do ye know what's goin' to come wit' the sun?
Sealers, b'ys. Fifteen hundred sealers from nine ships scourin' the ice
Lookin' for every man jack of us.

> PETER Lamb stares at MULLOWNEY, then tries to dance along.

**PETER**

I fell in a while back, and I'm wonderful cold.
It's time for bed, b'ys.
Help me off wit' me boots, won't ye?

**MULLOWNEY**

Go way, b'y. You're off the friggin' head.

**MCCARTHY**

There's the pot callin' the kettle black. Christ.

*PETER sits, struggles with a boot, dies where he sits. MULLOWNEY resumes his solitary waltz.*

**MCCARTHY**

That makes twelve gone here.

**DAWSON**

What about the other watches George? George?

**TUFF**

What? I don't know. Too many.
The young fellas playin' tag to stay warm is startin' to drop.
Them and the poor souls that fell in.

*BILLY trembles. DAWSON puts an arm around him.*

**DAWSON**

Andrew. Simon. Keep young Billy movin'.

**MCCARTHY**

I'd give me left nut for a cup of hot tea.

**LEVI**

There's no call for smut.

**MULLOWNEY**

Did ye ever see the beat of it, Mamie?
No. Nor me neither. All these fellas here to see ye.
George, b'y. Come take a turn with the missus.

**TUFF**

Lord God Jesus.

**LEVI**

God and Jesus is my best friends. George?
C'mon my son. What's a man wit'out a bit of hope?

*TUFF kneels by LEVI.*

**LEVI/TUFF**

God and Jesus is my best friends; they stands by me as I stands by them.

**TUFF**

If ever I needed thee, Jesus, 'tis now–

**MCCARTHY**

Hail Holy Queen–

**LEVI**

Our father which art in heaven–

**MCCARTHY**

Mother of Mercy–

**LEVI**

'Allowed be thy name. Thy kingdom come–

**MCCARTHY**

Hail our life, our sweetness and our hope–

**LEVI**

Simon! Andrew!

**TUFF/TEMPLEMANS**

Thy will be done, on earth as it is in 'eaven.

**LEVI**

Come on, Protestants! Praise the Lord in prayer!
(*raising volume*)
Give us this day our daily bread–

**MCCARTHY**

Come on, b'ys. For the Holy Father.
(*increased volume*)
Turn, then, most gracious advocate–

**CATHOLICS**

Thine eyes of mercy toward us–

**PROTESTANTS**

Forgive us our trespasses as we–

**MCCARTHY**

Louder!

**CATHOLICS**

(*shouted*)
And after this our exile, show unto us the blessed fruit of thy womb, Jesus.

**LEVI**

Smut merchant! Take yer 'eathen gibberish to the other side of the rafter.

**MCCARTHY**

Heathen gibberish, is it? The most beautiful words ever uttered.
Ye tight arsed, Godless black Protestant. Get to the other side yerself.

**LEVI**

No. Roman idolater. We will not.

**MCCARTHY**

Yes ye will.

**SIMON**

It'll take a better man than ye, Richard McCarthy.

**MCCARTHY**

Try yer luck wit' the strongest man on the ice.
Thomas. Step forward.

**TUFF**

B'ys, cool yer heels. Tom.
I believe I got a crow to pick wit' ye.

**DAWSON**

If I picks it, Tuff, ye'll damn well eat it. Step aside.

**TUFF**

No. I will not.

**DAWSON**

Alright. Every man in the fleet knows ye was promoted to Second Hand
Because ye're a brown-nosin' arse-kissin' yes man–

*A pathetic fight among weak men; TUFF and LEVI together are a
match for DAWSON. MCCARTHY cuts LEVI from the trio, lands
a blow. LEVI staggers.*

**LEVI**

Give me one good crack at that filthy mouth, sweet Jesus.
Richard McCarthy. Retract your filth–

*MCCARTHY flattens LEVI.*

**MCCARTHY**

Let that be a lesson on ye, ye moralizing old–

*SIMON and ANDREW take on MCCARTHY. MOULAND copies on.*

### MOULAND
Tuff. Dawson. Are ye civilized men?
Or a pack of roaring, racketin' animals?

> *MULLOWNEY forces MOULAND to the edge with the gaff spear. He begins to prod.*

### MULLOWNEY
Touch my Mamie one more time and I swear to God–

### MOULAND
You crazy bastard. I never even met yer blessed Mamie.

> *MOULAND seizes the gaff, breaks it over MULLOWNEY's back. He takes MULLOWNEY to the ice, pins then beats him mercilessly with his fists.*

### MULLOWNEY
Help! Murder!

### MOULAND
Shut yer damn trap.

### MULLOWNEY
Ah, Mamie. Help!

### MOULAND
Or I'll shut it for ye.

### MULLOWNEY
Murder–

### TUFF
Art. Get a holt of yerself.
You'll kill the poor mad creature.

> *MOULAND takes DAWSON, who's gotten TUFF by the throat, to the ice. LEVI hauls TUFF, MOULAND and DAWSON apart.*

### LEVI
Damned fools... wastin' our precious...
God forgive us for a pack of fools.

### MOULAND
George. Tom. Come wit' me.

### BILLY
Skipper Tom?

**DAWSON**

I'm alright Billy. Give us a hand to me feet.

**TUFF**

Collins! Get them boys movin' like ye did on the ship.
Get them singin' or marchin' or dancin' – any damn thing at all.

**MCCARTHY**

Except religion or politics.

**MOULAND**

Jesus, Tom... your feet.

**COLLINS**

Boys! We're goin' fishin'.
Line up, now, on the edge of the pan.
Great day, ain't it, what? Calm as a clock.
Hand out yer lines, boys. That's it.
The fish's runnin' somethin' wonderful.
That's the idea. Keep movin'.
Andrew! Sing us somethin' soothin'.

**LEVI**

Andrew! "Star of Logy Bay."

**ANDREW**

Yes Father.
(*sings*)
Ye ladies and ye gentlemen\ I pray ye lend an ear
While I locates the residence\ Of a lovely charmer fair.

**BILLY**

My face... me face is on fire. Andrew? Andrew?

**LEVI**

Andrew. See to young Billy. Simon!

**SIMON**

(*sings*)
The curling of her yellow hair\ First stole my heart away
And her place of 'abitation\ Is down in Logy Bay.

**COLLINS**

Everybody! Keep jiggin', b'ys.
It's a dandy day altogether.

*SEALERS continue to hum "Logy Bay" under the following scenes.*

**MOULAND**

That was about as shameful as it gets.

**TUFF**

Wasn't bad as all that. Got our blood movin'.
You got a wicked left, Dawson.

**MOULAND**

I always took pride in bein' the fella that bends in the wind.
I finally snapped.

**DAWSON**

We're hardly men at all any more.

**MOULAND**

What keeps ye goin', George?

**TUFF**

I got to get every man, dead or alive, back to our ship.

**MOULAND**

Nothin' more? Nothin' in yer own heart?

**TUFF**

What's in me heart's me own business.

**MOULAND**

Fair enough.

**TUFF**

I'm not an educated man. Nor am I a fool.
I was gave the strength to live.
Live I will for live I must.
If I lets go of that, I'm a gonner.

**DAWSON**

I wants to look old man Kean in the eye,
And call him a murderin' son of a bitch.

**MOULAND**

Nothin' kills a good man's soul quick as hatred, Thomas.

**DAWSON**

I only felt the lack of one thing in life.
Poverty and circumstance cheated me of a good education.
Billy Pear and them is smart as whips.
They needs a new father. Mary Clare allows I could be that man.
God help me, Art. Set me down.
I can't stand the pressure on these poor feet...

*DAWSON sits. The men have tired of COLLIN's cod jigging game.*

### COLLINS

Alright, men. We're at a time, now, in the parish hall.
The women ain't showed up for some queer reason.
The music's playin', it's warm as toast in here.
There's a swally on the go; the fiddler's crankin' out a waltz.
We're goin' to pair off, me sons, and dance.
Simon! Give us another verse, will ye?

### SIMON

It was a summer's evening\ This little place I found
I met her ancient father\ Who did me sore confound.

### COLLINS

Come on, boys! Everybody.

*The men waltz.*

### ENSEMBLE

If ye address my daughter\ I'll send her far away
And never she'll return again\ While ye're in Logy Bay.

*As they waltz, their humming underscores the following: In the lee of the pinnacle, BILLY Pear cuts at his left hand with his gaff head spike.*

### ANDREW

Billy, stop it.

### BILLY

Some of the fellas come up here for a joke, see, and took me hand.
They put this hard froze' thing in it's place

### ANDREW

What thing?

### BILLY

They carved this thing out of ice, set it afire and stuck it on me arm, here,
Where me left hand's supposed to be.
Why would they do that, Andrew?

### ANDREW

Billy, stop it.

*At some distance.*

### TUFF

Stand up if ye can, Tom b'y.
The men can't look up to ye when ye're lyin' down.

**DAWSON**

(*he tries, fails*)
They'd best look elsewhere.
Me feet and hands is gone numb altogether, b'ys.
Me joints is seizin' up.

**MOULAND**

You've got to try to stand, Thomas.

*DAWSON struggles to his knees. SIMON waltzes with LEVI.*

**SIMON**

Oh now I'll go a-roaming/ I can no longer stay
I'll search the wide world over/ In every town and bay
I'll search in vain through France and Spain/ Likewise Americ-a...

*LEVI stumbles, falls to the ice.*

**DAWSON**

Jesus. Levi's down.

*SIMON helps his father to his feet.*

**DAWSON**

Promise ye'll look out for young Billy if anythin' should happen to me.

**MOULAND**

You get to your feet, I'll look out for the boy.

**DAWSON**

Stand me up.
(*screams*)
Set me down. For Christ's sake set me down.

**TUFF**

Don't desert us, Tom b'y.

*ANDREW restrains BILLY.*

**ANDREW**

Slip yer hand under your right arm, to warm it. That's it.

*BILLY gashes his face.*

Billy, no. Father? Father!

*JESSOP steps from behind the pinnacle.*

**JESSOP**

What's the matter, little brother?

**ANDREW**

Billy's cuttin' at himself.
His cheeks is burnin'; he thinks his hand is ice.

**BILLY**

They put this burnin' ice thing where my left hand should be.
Now they're doin' the same thing to me nose and cheeks.

**ANDREW**

Who? Billy. Who?

**BILLY**

I don't know. Maybe the beast.
Help me get it off, won't ye, Jessop?

**JESSOP**

Give it over, Billy.

**BILLY**

What?

**JESSOP**

Your gaff head. Give it to me.

**BILLY**

I can't go home wit'out me gaff head. I'll be pitied...
Look. See? It's not my hand.
When I cuts it, it don't even bleed.
I'm not dead, am I?

**JESSOP**

You might be better off dead than goin' home crippled, Billy.

**BILLY**

No. Would I?

**JESSOP**

Why burden yer poor mother wit' a another mouth to feed?

**ANDREW**

Jessop. Get away.
Billy. You're not going to die.

**BILLY**

Take it, Andrew.

**ANDREW**

Thank you.

**BILLY**

You're welcome.
I t'inks if ye could just make a cut along there... -

**ANDREW**

(*drops the gaff head, runs*)
Father! Father!

**JESSOP**

You're lucky ye grew up wit' no father.
(*hands BILLY the gaff head*)
Here now, Billy. Don't look at me.

**BILLY**

Are ye the beast?

**JESSOP**

Like father, like son.
Don't look at me.

> *The waltzing and humming stops. BILLY cuts at his face. Blood. JESSOP exits.*

**TUFF**

We can't be far from a ship.

**MOULAND**

There's more snow to drift, now.
We'll spend the day if this wind don't drop.

**TUFF**

You'll hear the Admiral's men singin' out like birds at sunrise.

**DAWSON**

He thinks we're aboard of the *Newfoundland*, George.
There's no wireless to tell him any different.
No one knows we're out.

**ANDREW**

Jessop said poor Billy's good as dead.

**LEVI**

Jessop was 'ere?

**ANDREW**

Don't let 'im die, father.

**LEVI**

Dawson. Get over 'ere and look out for that youngster.
Keep yer wits about ye, Andrew.
Ye and Simon got to git 'ome to yer mother.

**TUFF**

If ye don't rise, ye're done for.
On yer feet, Dawson.

> *With their help, DAWSON rises. They walk DAWSON to BILLY;*
> *DAWSON's progress is labourious, agonizing.*

**ANDREW**

Billy. Can ye hear me?

**BILLY**

(*sings*)
I loves to sit be'... be'–

**LEVI**

Andrew, come away.

**ANDREW**

No.
(*sings*)
Be' the big black stove...

**BILLY**

(*sings*)
Be' the big black stove...

**ANDREW**

That's right Billy. You're safe to home. Warm and happy.
(*sings*)
An' watch the kittle bilin'/ Billy's gonna buy me a new silk dress/
When he comes home from swilin'.

**BILLY**

(*sings*)
An' watch the kittle... when I gets home from–

**DAWSON**

Billy?

**BILLY**

I'm all bloody. Mother? Wash me...

*BILLY dies.*

**DAWSON**

Aw, Jesus. Billy.

**MOULAND**

Come away, Thomas. Come away.

**DAWSON**

(*sits*)
Leave me be.

**SIMON**

Father? Me ears is stopped burning.

**LEVI**

(*unwinds scarf*)
Take this.

**SIMON**

Leave it round yer neck where mother put it.
Me ears was way too big anyway.

**ANDREW**

Billy never hurt a soul in his life. Jessop come and–

**LEVI**

"The dyin' shall live, the livin' shall die..."
Simon...? I forgets the rest...

**SIMON**

"And spirits shall, untune the sky."

**ANDREW**

He was like a cat wit' a mouse.

*DAWSON lowers himself to the ice.*

**TUFF**

Tom.

**DAWSON**

I can't go home to Mary Clare wit'out her young Billy.

**TUFF**

How will it be for her to lose the both of ye?
You got to live, if ye loves her at all.

**DAWSON**

How am I to care for her?
Cripplin' around the house, more monster than man.
She'll find someone else, and be the better for it.

**TUFF**

How can I tell Admiral Kean I lost the strongest man on the ice?

**DAWSON**

I doubt he'll miss me too severe.
Our fight's wit' ourselves now, George b'y. Not each other.
Put one foot in front of the other long as ye can, my son.
When ye can't, have the good sense to lie down.
Don't blame the fallen, b'ys.
The strongest of men is no match for this.
Get poor Billie to shelter.

*ANDREW is racked by violent shivers.*

**LEVI**

Art. Keep them boys of mine up and movin'.
Do ye hear what I'm sayin'?

**MOULAND**

I do.
Alright. Listen to me. Every fella step behind me in a line. Tha's it. C'mon.
Thump the fella in front, all around where the neck meets the shoulders.
We'll take a slow march to warm our feet.

**SIMON**

Come on, Skipper.

**LEVI**

I'll mark time here until I gets limbered up a bit.

**ANDREW**

Father.

**LEVI**

Go on, now. I'll be there in a minute.

**MOULAND**

Andrew. Simon. Get over here.
George, take over, will ye?
I gotta get back to my men.

> *ANDREW and SIMON join the back of the line. JESSOP enters. Using MOULAND's gaff as a staff, JESSOP pushes his brothers into the black water. LEVI struggles to the edge.*

**LEVI**

Andrew! Simon!
Take me 'ands. Name of Jesus, take me 'ands.
Help! Somebody grab a holt of me or I'm gone too.

> *ANDREW and SIMON are pulled onto the pan. LEVI stands them on their feet, holds them to him, an arm around each.*

**JESSOP**

There now. The perfect picture.

**LEVI**

Devil.

**JESSOP**

You might as well eat the meat as drink the gravy.

**MOULAND**

You killed your brothers.

**JESSOP**

I never knowed heaven and hell was the same place,
Mixed up together, all around us, right here on earth.
I knows now. Thanks to ye, Skipper Art.

**MOULAND**

I told ye something else entirely.

**LEVI**

What did ye say to that boy?

**MOULAND**

I don't know... a lot of things. Nothing.

**LEVI**

What did you say!

**JESSOP**

I never knowed how miserable I was 'till ye showed me.

**MOULAND**

He twisted my words. God help me. I can't remember.

**JESSOP**

The sun's risin' through the drift, father.
You'll never see it set.

**MOULAND**

Gimme me gaff or I'll knock ye down.

**JESSOP**

The saint's got some sinner in him after all.

*JESSOP exits into darkness. ANDREW and SIMON slump. LEVI bears them up.*

**LEVI**

You'd 'a spared our good name, Mouland,
By shovin' us into the water yerself.
Come on, me sons.
There's no more fish in these waters.
We're headin' in.
Simon. Keep her nose into the wind.

*ANDREW slumps. LEVI rights him.*

**LEVI**

We're well passed Kreelman's Rock, Andrew.
Look sharp, my son.
Keep an eye out for the Grinders.

*SIMON falls. LEVI bears him up.*

**MULLOWNEY**

Ah, Mamie. Ye know the queerest thing ever I seen?
Me. I was never so happy or clear in me own mind.
Them poor fools, goin' down to the ice to die.
I showed them the way we danced on the night we become...
They was too blind to see what we was to each other.
Poor devils. They never seen you, my Mamie.
Rouse the youngsters and send them to me, will you my dear?
(*He kneels, sits, then eases himself to the ice.*)
Look at ye. Beautiful, beautiful children.
Did ye ever see the beat of it?
Tender and precious as life itself.
Jenny, me dear. And darlin' little Michael.
Come sit be' yer poor father.
Sing me somethin'. Yes. D'as it.
Yer angels. Precious angels 'a God.

*MULLOWNEY dies.*

**LEVI**

We'll be found standin' upright, not flat on our backs .
Stay on yer feet and face the wind, b'ys.
"Make me hear joy and gladness,
That the bones which Thou 'ast broken may rejoice.
For thou desirest not sacrifices; else I would give it."

    *SIMON dies.*

**LEVI**

Please God.
*(holds him upright)*
Not our Simon.

**JESSOP**

*(off)*
Father!

**LEVI**

Too 'ard, Lord. Too 'ard.

    *ANDREW dies.*

**LEVI**

Oh, Jesus!

    *LEVI dies. The trio, LEVI and his sons, stand immobile, LEVI holding*
    *each upright, facing the wind.*

**MOULAND**

Has anyone a gaff? How am I to lead wit' no gaff?

    *MOULAND exits. Lem COLLINS approaches George TUFF.*

**COLLINS**

Skipper George?

**TUFF**

Leave me be.

**COLLINS**

I needs to talk to ye... what do ye make of it?

**TUFF**

You'd do well to go and find yerself a place to die.

**COLLINS**

I'm not goin' to die.

**TUFF**

I don't think there'll be a man left to tell the tale.
(*He weeps.*)
We're all goin' to smother.
We're all goin' to perish.
Where are ye going?

**COLLINS**

Far from ye as I can.

**TUFF**

You asked a question, I'm tellin' ye the truth.

**COLLINS**

I'm not goin' to die.

**TUFF**

Maybe not. But ye'd best prepare yer spirit.

**COLLINS**

I come to ye for hope. Ye tell me to get ready to die.
I come for strength. Ye weaken me.
What kind of leader are ye?

**TUFF**

Lemuel. Lem. Come back.

**COLLINS**

What?

**TUFF**

Is that the sun?

**COLLINS**

Yes.

**TUFF**

Not the moon?

**COLLINS**

No.

**TUFF**

Then it is day. Is there a ship near?

**COLLINS**

I can't see through the drift.

**TUFF**

If we can't see them, they can't see us.
Hoist me up the pinnacle.
If I get above the drift, I may see a ship.

*Climbs to COLLIN's shoulders, braced by the pinnacle.*

**TUFF**

Thank God.

**COLLINS**

What do ye see, Skipper?

**TUFF**

Ships froze in the ice. To every point of the compass.

**COLLINS**

How far?

**TUFF**

The *Bellaventure*'s near.
All the pretty lights.

*A flood of light... sunrise.*

(*hand to eyes*)
Agh! Jesus.
(*tumbles to the ice*)
Give us yer arm...
Take me to Arthur.
Art, b'y! Art!
Perk up, me son!
We're not a mile from a warm bunk and a good meal.
We're goin' home.

## ACT THREE

*Wind. Brilliant sunlight. George TUFF, alone.*

### TUFF
All the pretty lights.
Collins? Lemuel Collins?
Jesus God in Heaven.
Look at me.
All them years workin' like the dog for Captain Kean and *Newfoundland.*
I finally saves enough to commence makin' somethin' of meself.
Start me own family:
Find the time to learn to read a book;
Show me intent by writing George Tuff
Instead of marking down a God-forsaken X.
No sir. The back of your hand fer poor George Tuff.
Is that what I am to ye?
A God-forsaken creature to rise up or strike down as ye sees fit?
Maybe ye're doin' right.
A man can loose his own way and no harm done.
But to lead other souls astray...
Lord God, forgive me.
Leaving that compass aboard of the *Stephano...*
The worst thing I ever done.
Now ye're set to snuff this poor little light of mine entirely, ain't ye?
What pleasure does ye take in this?
I thought ye was s'possed to be merciful.
There's something poison in ye.
You're no better – God forgive me–
Ye're no better than Captain Abram Kean hisself!
There. I said it. Only nobody heard.
Well sir. Ye might be done wit' me.
But I ain't.
Not by a damn sight.
Who's there?
Is anyone there?

### COLLINS
*(enters)*
None living.

### TUFF
Slit open me pocket. Go ahead.
Now take and put me snow glasses on me.
Am I right in sayin' the drift's abated?

### COLLINS
There's only wind.

### TUFF

Why did ye run out on me, Lem? Lem?
(*silence*)
Give me yer hand...
Take me to a man wit' a pair of overalls on 'e.
We'll cut them off to make a flag.

### COLLINS

He's lookin' at me.

### TUFF

Who?

### COLLINS

Theopholis Chaulk.

### TUFF

Poor Theoph died at dawn. His lookin' days is over.

### COLLINS

His eyes is wide open. There's sparkle... he ain't dead.

### TUFF

'Tis only frost. What kind of drawers is 'e wearin'?

### COLLINS

"Ye was such a good lad, Lem me son," he says.
"Don't be thievin' me overalls and it so cold...
What made ye turn so hard?"

### TUFF

What made him turn so hard is more like it.
Is he wearin' wool under?
Or that damn new American cotton stuff.

### COLLINS

Cotton.

### TUFF

I told Captain Kean that stuff was no damn good for this climate.
"Oh, no," he says. "It's the latest thing, George b'y.
Lighter than wool and just as warm.
The men'll be snug enough. The merchants'll turn an honest dollar.
Our American friends will be happy and trade will flourish."
That's what the old bugger said. "Trade will flourish."
Why did ye run out on me?

**COLLINS**

I sought out me cousins, Hez and Peter Seward.
I was that lonesome for family.

**TUFF**

Fix the overalls to me gaff as a flag stick.

**COLLINS**

They was lyin' on the ice, pressed together like spoons.
They was singin'. Honest to God they was singin'.

**TUFF**

There's nothing like wool right next to the skin
When a fella works up a lather on a blowey day.

**COLLINS**

I kindled a bit of fire from Peter's haul rope.
I cut open their molasses can. Made them a hot drink.

**TUFF**

I'd give a dollar note for every man still alive,
Wearin' that cursed Yankee fleece.

**COLLINS**

I roused them up. They walked about for a spell, jokin' and laughin'.
I thought I'd cheated the cold of their lives.
Of a sudden they dropped to the ice as one.
Passed from existence wit' no word for meself or family.

**TUFF**

Are ye done?

**COLLINS**

No. I believe the sudden heat of the drink was too much fer them.
I never meant to. But I believe I killed them.
What'll I say to their poor mother?

**TUFF**

Nothin' if we ain't spotted. Are ye finished?

**COLLINS**

Yes.

**TUFF**

Climb the pinnacle.

**COLLINS**

I can't.

**TUFF**

Then put me to the pinnacle and climb me.

*TUFF embraces the pinnacle. COLLINS climbs him.*

**TUFF**

What do ye see?

**COLLINS**

The *Bellaventure*, sou'west. Mouland and McCarthy's close.
Out in the open on a new sheet of smooth ice.

*In the middle distance, the sudden rev of engines.*

**COLLINS**

Mouland's found a jersey for a flag.
Wave 'er, Art! Tha's it. Wave yer flag!

**TUFF**

Lem?

**COLLINS**

Run, Art. Run!
(*laughter*)
That's the queerest sight I ever seen.

**TUFF**

What?

**COLLINS**

Art Mouland tryin' to flap his wings.
Like a fly in brine!
(*laughter fades*)
Oh, God.

**TUFF**

What?

**COLLINS**

Art's down.
The wind got him.
Jesus God 'a mercy.
McCarthy's down too.

**TUFF**

Down? What?
On the ice?
Lem?
What happened?

#### COLLINS

They just... blowed away.
Slid topsy turvy,
Like rag dolls pitched across't a polished floor by a angry child.

#### TUFF

What are ye doing?

#### COLLINS

Blindin' sun. Bluest kinda' sky.
There's a layer of glass... no... must be ice...
Clear fresh ice an inch thick on everything.
And diamonds... I never seen it so pretty.

#### TUFF

Pretty is as pretty does. What else do ye see?

#### COLLINS

I sees the *Newfoundland* to the southeast.

#### TUFF

How far?

#### COLLINS

Not more than a mile. The *Bell*'s steamin' nor' east at a fair clip.

#### TUFF

Where's the *Stephano* to?

#### COLLINS

Nor' west.

#### TUFF

How far?

#### COLLINS

A little ways off.
God 'a mercy. She's steamin' in this direction.

#### TUFF

Are ye sure?

#### COLLINS

Certain.

#### TUFF

The flag. Captain Kean seen my flag.

**COLLINS**

No. There's a pan of pelts. And men.

**TUFF**

How far?

**COLLINS**

If I could shout, they could hear me.

**TUFF**

Then for Christ's sake shout.

**COLLINS**

(*croaks*)
Capt– Admira– Help–

**TUFF**

Wave yer arms. Do they see ye?

**COLLINS**

No. They're slingin' pelts aboard.

**TUFF**

He'll load the pelts then come get us.

MOULAND *enters.*

**MOULAND**

I wisht I'd 'a had a sail.
I wisht the wind would'a took me way up in the air
And dropped me down in Hare Bay.
I'd knock. The door'd open. There she'd be. My Belle.
She'd say–

**TUFF**

Who's there?

**COLLINS**

Art and Richard.

**TUFF**

B'ys, cheer up.
We seen Captain Kean comin' on slow, pickin' out a good lead.
Who's comin' wit' me to the *Stephano*?
(*silence*)
Lem? Gimme yer arm. That's the boy.

TUFF *exits led by Lem* COLLINS. MCCARTHY *enters.*

#### MCCARTHY
There's somethin' queer about Tuff.

#### MOULAND
He's snow blind.

> *Sunset casts long red/gold shadows. Cries of cows and pups break the*
> *silence. Gunshot crack of new ice splitting. Reverberation.*

#### MOULAND
What's that?

#### MCCARTHY
Time, me son. Time just fell to the ice and shattered.

> *MCCARTHY walks among the dead.*

#### MCCARTHY
Fifteen last night. Twelve this mornin'. Eight so far this afternoon.

#### MOULAND
You're some ghoulish, forever countin' the dead.

#### MCCARTHY
If I can still count, I knows I'm not among them.

#### MOULAND
Look at us. Steppin' over them like so much drift wood.

#### MCCARTHY
William Lawlor fell beside me first light.
I took' no more interest than if I'd 'a dropped me pipe.

#### MOULAND
Nature's changed in us.

#### MCCARTHY
Listen.

#### MOULAND
I don't hear nothin'.

#### MCCARTHY
The ringin' in me ears... gone, b'y. The wind is dropped.

#### MOULAND
Silence. Thanks be to God.

### MCCARTHY
What time do ye make 'er?

*A cow calls to her pup. The pup responds. Silence.*

### MOULAND
You're the man wit' the watch.

*Distant engines, very faint. COLLINS enters.*

### COLLINS
If Kean'd turned his head ten degrees he'd 'a seen us.
I turns and there's Skipper George.
Stuck outa the ice; cut off, in the middle.
'E stumbled into a swile's breathin' hole, see...

*Enter George TUFF.*

### TUFF
Nobody knows we're here.
She steamed away.
Nobody knows we're here...

### COLLINS
Poor Skipper George.
Starin' at the ship, mumblin' the same thing over and over.

### TUFF
Nobody knows we're here. Nobody knows–

### MOULAND
George b'y.

### TUFF
I'm in charge here, Tom Dawson.

### MOULAND
George, it's Art Mouland.
Ye took an awful shock, b'y.

### TUFF
You got a damn annoyin' mouth on ye, Dawson.

### MOULAND
You fell in.

### TUFF
You've been hard against me from the day we left St. John's town.

**MOULAND**

Tom Dawson's dead. You'll be too, if ye don't take a holt.

**TUFF**

The Admiral thinks we're safe on the *Newfoundland* wit' Captain Wes.
Captain Wes thinks we're wit' his father.
We're lost thirty hours already.
Nobody knows we're here.
How'll we make it through another night?
Answer me that?
We're all gonna smother, b'ys.
(*weeps*)
We're all gonna perish.

**MOULAND**

George. I want ye to take a holt of young Lem Collins.

**COLLINS**

Jinker! Get him away from me.

**TUFF**

Tom Dawson's the strongest man on the ice.

**MOULAND**

Lemuel.

**COLLINS**

What?

**MOULAND**

I want ye and George to walk over to the edge of the pan.
Right over there. Do ye see where I'm pointing to?

**TUFF**

Plain as day.
(*takes Lemuel COLLINS' arm*)
Why wouldn't I?

**MOULAND**

Good. When ye get there, turn around and come back.
Then take and do the same again.
Me and McCarthy'll be right behind ye.
It's yer job to show us the way and our job to follow.

**COLLINS**

Come on Skipper George.

**TUFF**

Alright, boys.

**COLLINS**

Let's take a stroll down be' the harbour.

**TUFF**

Take me down be' the harbour, Lem.

**COLLINS**

Mind the rocks, Skipper. Step up. And over.
(*stepping over fallen sealers*)
That's the idea.

**MOULAND**

Keep movin'... tha's it. Portion out yer strength.

**TUFF**

Keep moving.

**MOULAND**

We got a long night ahead.

**MCCARTHY**

Jesus. I wonder ye got Tuff back.

**MOULAND**

He may be blind as a bat; he's also tough as a boiled owl.
I 'spose 'e just needs a sense of purpose... like the rest of us.
Queer, 'though, ain't it?

**MCCARTHY**

What's that?

**MOULAND**

It don't seem to matter what that purpose is.

> *Nightfall. Cold. Silent. Still. Brilliant starlight. The full moon rises, hangs low on the horizon.*

**MOULAND**

What's the first thing ye'll do when ye gets aboard of the *Newfoundland*?

**MCCARTHY**

A tub of warm water and a plate of beans'd go down some nice.

**MOULAND**

George?

**TUFF**

Sleep. Just sleep.

**COLLINS**

First thing I'll do is wire my Daisy.

**TUFF**

Why would ye do that?

**COLLINS**

Tell her I'm all right.

**TUFF**

You mustn't upset her for no reason.

**COLLINS**

What do ye mean?

**TUFF**

She don't know ye're in trouble.

**MOULAND**

Keep movin' boys.

**TUFF**

Boiled dinner...
The t'ought makes a warm glow in me belly.

**MOULAND**

It's the salt meat ye're hankerin' after?

**TUFF**

No, b'y. Two or three cups of steamin' broth.

**MCCARTHY**

Potatoes. Peas pudding.

**TUFF**

Cabbage. Carrots.

**MOULAND**

Big chunks of that illegal moose I shot yesterday.

**TUFF**

Arthur. Ye was out here yesterday.

**MOULAND**

Oh. Yes. This'll be our second night.

**MCCARTHY**

Yes, b'y. Have a t'ought to keep yer wits about ye.

**TUFF**

Tea wit' canned milk. Oh my yes. Hot milky tea.
Slab of bangbelly wit' jam onto it.

**MCCARTHY**

Fire in the kitchen. The missus washin' the youngsters.
Them pink in the lamp light. Me watchin'.
Driftin' off on the day bed, be' the hot stove. Her wakin' me...

**MOULAND**

(*sings*)
I loves to sit be' the big black stove.../ An watch the kittle bilin'...
Poor young Billy.

**TUFF**

Arthur. Richard. Keep movin'.

**COLLINS**

If my Daisy don't know I'm okay, in me own mind I'm not.

**MCCARTHY**

One sardine, froze hard as a nut.
Collins. Share this little fish wit' Tuff.
One piece of excursion bread.
That'll be our supper, Art.

**MOULAND**

Not our last, I hopes.

**MCCARTHY**

Loaves and fishes, b'y. Loaves and fishes.

**MOULAND**

It'll take a miracle to get it down me t'roat.
There's neither heat nor spit left in me.

**MCCARTHY**

I'll chew for ye.

**MOULAND**

I'm goin' to say something.
Ye got to tell me if I'm right or wrong, or off me head entire.
Time is quarts and pints. Not feet and inches. Right or wrong?

**MCCARTHY**

What?

#### MOULAND

Time is volume. Round, like an orange...
Not straight lines. Like a ruler, say, or a yardstick.
Right or wrong?

#### MCCARTHY

Yer off your head entire. Open up.

*MCCARTHY feeds MOULAND chewed food.*

#### TUFF

Is there moonlight, Lem?

#### COLLINS

She's full. I'll be damned if I'll sit here and perish. Who's comin'?

#### TUFF

A fella'd best decide where it is e's goin' before 'e sets out.
Boys, we're goin to elevate young Lemuel here.

*They push COLLINS up the pinnacle.*

#### TUFF

What do ye see?

#### COLLINS

Village lights across the harbour...

#### TUFF

We're forty miles from shore, Lem.

#### COLLINS

No. Ships. It'd be ships. I sees the *Newfoundland*. Do I?
I does. The walkin' couldn't be better, Skipper.

#### TUFF

We're goin' for her.

#### MCCARTHY

I wouldn't. Not 'till daylight.

#### TUFF

What if daylight comes too late?

#### MCCARTHY

Keep out of them breathin' holes.

#### TUFF

Don't be talkin'. Lem?

**COLLINS**

Yes Skipper.

**TUFF**

Give me yer arm. You and me is takin' a little moonlight stroll.

**COLLINS**

Yes sir, Skipper George.

*They exit. MCCARTHY finds shelter leeward of the pinnacle.*

**MOULAND**

Christ.

**MCCARTHY**

What?

**MOULAND**

Monkeys. Flyin' around me head.
Dirty damn monkeys eatin' up every sane thought that comes to me.

**MCCARTHY**

Art. Come over here and set a spell. Arthur!
Ye never told what ye'd do when ye got home.

**MOULAND**

Fall on me knees. Lay me head against my dear Belle's stomach.
Listen for the sound of my child's beatin' heart.

*Enter JESSOP, carrying MOULAND's gaff.*

**MOULAND**

You're come back fer me, ain't ye? Ain't ye!

**JESSOP**

Your pup is dead.

**MOULAND**

What?

**JESSOP**

Your wife is dead.

**MOULAND**

No. Me and Belle, we only just found each other–

**MCCARTHY**

Art. Come in out of it.

#### JESSOP
She died givin' birth to yer dead runt of a monkey baby.

#### MOULAND
No!

#### MCCARTHY
Art?

#### MOULAND
Are ye the devil. Or are ye real?

#### JESSOP
Who says the devil ain't real?
I come to take back me property.
I needs yer knife. I'll trade fer yer gaff.

#### MOULAND
T'row it on the ice before me and step away back.

#### JESSOP
T'row the knife first.

#### MOULAND
No, b'y. Once burned...

#### JESSOP
Twice shy. Here. Take yer damned gaff. I'm t'rough wit' it.

> *The exchange is made. JESSOP cuts at LEVI's pants pocket.*

#### MCCARTHY
Look at the moon. She's tinged red.

#### JESSOP
(*removes LEVI's watch*)
He promised me this when I was child.
Now he tells me Simon's more deservin'.

> *Male voices, the sealers; choral tones, harmonic, then diffused, dissonant.*
> *LEVI breaks his stance.*

#### LEVI
Jessop!

#### MOULAND
Answer yer father.

**JESSOP**

Me father's dead.

**LEVI**

Jessop. Come stand wit' me and yer brothers.

**MOULAND**

Ask his forgiveness.

**JESSOP**

For freein' us from his cursed tyranny? Why would I.
The old brute's dead.

**MOULAND**

Levi? He can't see ye.
I can.
Am I dead or alive?

**LEVI**

Caught between two shores, b'y.

**MOULAND**

Wit' no way home.

**LEVI**

Where there's a will, my son.... Look here.
Billy! Sit up, Billy.

> BILLY Pear rises. His face, hands and naked chest glisten with blood.

**BILLY**

Look at me, Skipper. Covered in blood.
How's that? I never even killed me first seal.

**LEVI**

It's yer own blood Billy.

**MOULAND**

I thought you was safe at home.

**BILLY**

I got lost. Skipper Tom?
Get up. Someone got to show me the way.

**LEVI**

No, Billy. Leave the dead lie in peace.

**MOULAND**

His poor feet...

**BILLY**

You're the smartest man on the ice, Art.
Help me get Skipper Tom onto his feet.

**MOULAND**

Richard? McCarthy! Get over here.
There's a man and a boy standin' in front of me.

**MCCARTHY**

Two boys. Levi Templeman, froze solid.
Andrew and Simon, his two dead sons.

**BILLY**

Mam'll be some cross if I comes home wit'out ye, Skipper Tom.

**MOULAND**

It's Billy Pear. Levi raised him up.

**MCCARTHY**

Take a deep breath. Now heave it out of ye.
That cloud before ye? You're talkin' to yer own breath.

**BILLY**

I died last night, cuttin' at meself.
Wash me when ye gets me ashore, won't ye Skipper Art?

**MOULAND**

Ah, Billy.

**BILLY**

I can't be sent back to mother all covered in me own blood.

**LEVI**

Help the poor lad.

**MOULAND**

How am I to help him?

**BILLY**

I wants ye to tell mother I died quiet and calm.
Tell her I just went to sleep, not in the ragin' starm, but tonight.
When the moon and stars was bright...

**JESSOP**

When God and the Devil came home to the world.

**LEVI**

Go on home now, Billy. It's time you was in bed.

**BILLY**

She'll see me bloody.

**LEVI**

She seen ye bloody the day ye was born.
Tell her ye're 'appy and warm now.
Tell her not to worry.
Tell her ye died a good death.

**BILLY**

Tell her? Tell her how?

**LEVI**

Visit her dream.

**BILLY**

Wash me Skipper Art.

**MOULAND**

It won't come off.

**BILLY**

Wash me with your tears.

**MOULAND**

I've no more tears to—

**LEVI**

It's alright Billy. Back in bed with ye.
That's a good lad.

> BILLY lays down on the ice.

**MOULAND**

I promised Tom Dawson—

**LEVI**

He's safe, now. Snug in the old house up the hill from the 'arbour.
She keeps the house some good inside.
Fresh whitewash. Floors sparkling in the moonlight.
Listen. The little brother talks in his sleep;
"Mother," he says, clear as a bell...
"Our Billy's come home from the swiles."
My, my. The smell of the place, me son.

**MOULAND**

Pies and fresh bread?

**LEVI**

Yes. Waxed floors, just a shinin'.
Moon risin' through the lace curtains...
Tracin' fern and swallow patterns onto the parlour floor.
Who's she by the window, lookin' out the harbour, past the head...
Down the trail of moonlight, out to the sea of glass?
My, my. She's a beauty.

**MOULAND**

Belle?

**JESSOP**

Dead.

**MOULAND**

Liar! Send me home, Levi, like you done Billy.
In the name of God, I beg you. Send me home.

**LEVI**

You send me my son. I'll send you home.

**MOULAND**

Send...? Wha...?

*The choral tones fade. In the distance, engines rev.*

**MCCARTHY**

Listen. The *Newfoundland*!

**JESSOP**

You killed me Mouland.

**MOULAND**

I only tried to help–

**JESSOP** ˙

I could have been safe aboard of her by now.
You p'isoned me mind wit' doubt.

**LEVI**

"A good name is better than precious ointment."
Restore our good name, Mouland.
I want us found, the four of us, me and my three boys
Standing froze together.
Send me my Jessop and I'll send you home.

**MOULAND**

Home.

*The engines fade as distance grows.*

**MCCARTHY**

Stuck in the ice two full weeks.
Useless old tub. Now she's steamin' away.

**COLLINS**

(*enters*)
Come and sit a spell, Daisy my love.
What'll ye do if I gives you a kiss?
Come on, now me duckey.
Warm up me poor froze lips.

**TUFF**

(*off*)
Lem? Lemuel?! I'm lost...

**COLLINS**

Don't you move, Daisy. I got to look out for poor George Tuff.

*Tuff enters.*

**TUFF**

Lem? Lem Collins...

**COLLINS**

Daisy. This here's Skipper George.
He's a good enough fella. Ain't ye, Skipper? Skipper?
This here's my Daisy.

**TUFF**

Lem. Your Daisy's home in her bed.

**COLLINS**

If I can't have my Daisy, no one can.
Come here, Daisy me love.

*COLLINS removes his mitts.*

**MCCARTHY**

Tuff. Collins. Mitts...

**TUFF**

What?

**MCCARTHY**

Jesus, Lemuel. You'll never get them on again.

**COLLINS**

(*attempts to remove his cap*)
Me hats froze to the hairs of me head.
I must look some particular, do I Daisy?

> *Nearby, a seal pup's cry.*

**TUFF**

Did ye hear that?

> *SIMON and ANDREW stir; they jig cod with a slow, grave rhythm.*

**MOULAND**

Jessop said my baby died.

**ANDREW/SIMON**

(*sing*)
How could ye be so cruel as...

**MOULAND**

Died and took my Belle.

**ANDREW/SIMON**

(*sing*)
To part me from my love.

**LEVI**

He lied.

**TUFF**

Listen!

**MOULAND**

Why did ye lie to me?

**JESSOP**

(*exact echo*)
Why did ye lie to me?

**TUFF**

Listen. Listen!

> *Brisk and purposeful, LEVI mounts an angled, tabular rafter.*

**LEVI**

Come aboard, Art.

> *MOULAND struggles up.*

Look. Your Belle's alive.

#### MOULAND
Belle. Yes... I sees her. Levi? Our baby?

#### LEVI
Your little girl floats in the briniest of seas, dreamin' the start of her life.

#### MOULAND
A little girl. Belle'll be that pleased.

#### ANDREW/SIMON
(*sing*)
Her constant heart beats in her breast/
As tender as a dove.

#### LEVI
Do as I ask, and I'll give ye a sail.

#### MOULAND
A sail?

#### LEVI
The wind'll raise ye up, and drop ye in Hare Bay.
Your Belle will open the door.

#### ANDREW/SIMON
(*sing*)
Oh Venus was no fairer/
Or the lovely month of May.

#### MOULAND
"Welcome home my dear."
She'll hold me in her arms. She'll say–
"You're more to me than life itself."

> *A single vocal tone, another, and another; then harmonic choral tones establish, resonate. Dead sealers rise from the ice.*

#### TUFF
Shush. Just listen.... What's that?

#### MOULAND
The souls of the dead men.

#### LEVI
The prayers of the living.

**TUFF**

Lemuel! I hears a swile...

**JESSOP**

Mixed wit' the cries of the swiles. Pitiful.

**MOULAND**

Beautiful.

**LEVI**

The Harps of God.

**MOULAND**

I never seen such depth of stars. Never the moon so full.

**JESSOP**

Never the moon so red.

**MOULAND**

Too red.

**JESSOP**

Blood red.

**TUFF**

Lem?

**JESSOP**

Look. Shafts 'a light, curves like scythes, rises up...
One from either side.

**LEVI**

The great horns of the beast.

**JESSOP**

The beast afoot with two horns blazin'.

**SEALERS**

(*on the wind*)
Save us.

> *The vocal tones fade. Dead sealers drift off. The pup calls.*

**TUFF**

Lemuel?

**JESSOP**

Their cries is so pitiful.

### MOULAND

More pitiful than the cries of men?

*The pup's cry, nearer now.*

### LEVI

Seals in their plenty; God's blessing, to us and our children.

### COLLINS

If I perish, who'll marry me Daisy?

### TUFF

Lemuel. Let's find that swile pup.
We'll cuddle the poor thing between us for its warmth.

*TUFF and COLLINS exit. The tones re-establish, sustained, harsh, atonal.*

### MOULAND

What have we done to rouse the wrath of God?

### LEVI

Set ourselves above nature.

*The dead sealers enter, stand or move with no apparent purpose.*

### SEALERS

Save us, Art.
You're the man can...
Save us.

### MOULAND

Don't ye fear for yer immortal soul, Jessop?
After what ye done?

### JESSOP

I flew to the moon – queen of the seals.
Circled round, behind her back,
Where the devil tethers the two-horned beast;
I cut his tether, climbed on his back.
I rode the beast through hell 'till I found my father.
I asked his forgiveness.
He cursed my soul to wander this frozen waste, forever and alone.
Now he's dead. I'm that glad.
For the first time in my life, I am free.
I never felt better.

*Seal pup's cry distress. Cow responds; threat, anger.*

**MCCARTHY**

They have him. God save us. They got the pup.
Raise him up, George b'y! Tha's it!
Press him between ye, now. For his warmth!
God. Such heat they'll feel. Such heat.

**SEALERS**

Save us.

**MOULAND**

Set the poor creatures free, can't ye, Levi?

**LEVI**

Send me my Jessop. I'll set them free.
Then I'll bring ye to yer Belle.

**MOULAND**

Can my Belle hear me?

*The vocal tones, barely present, swell then diminish.*

**MOULAND**

Ah, Belle. I thought ye was dead.
Do ye feel it? All I want to do is sing out to God.
Am I to die here tonight?
Then fill my soul wit' love and send it home to me wife and child.
But if I lives... please, God. I begs ye.
Don't send me home a broken man.

**LEVI**

Raise yer gaff above my wicked boy's head.
Bring it down with all your force.

*The choral tones cut mid-phrase.*

**MOULAND**

No.

**LEVI**

Send that boy to stand with his brothers.

**MOULAND**

No!

**LEVI**

Poor fatherless child.
Is that what you want for your daughter?
You're hard-hearted, Mouland.

**MCCARTHY**

Thirst.

**SEALERS**

Thirst. Terrible thirst...

**MCCARTHY**

Worse than cold or hunger.

**SEALERS**

Cold. Terrible cold.

**MCCARTHY**

Cold as a merchant's heart.

**LEVI**

See his brothers, standing there, hard as stone?
They was my future.

**MCCARTHY**

Tuff. Kill the pup, can't ye?
His blood will slake our cravin.

**JESSOP**

Look at me. Look close. What do ye see?

**MOULAND**

I can't tell the difference between ye and...

**JESSOP**

We're that much alike.

**SEALERS**

Thirst. Terrible thirst.

> *The dead sealers press close around MOULAND and JESSOP.*

**SEALERS**

Save us.

> *The seal pup cries.*

**MOULAND**

God forgive me. I got to make one last kill.

> *MOULAND prods JESSOP with the gaff, forcing him toward the tabular rafter.*

### JESSOP

My blood for yours. Is that it Mouland?
I knew you'd look out for your own skin–

### MOULAND

They tells us when we're youngsters God is love.
Did they tell you that Jessop?
Now they says he went and left us stranded.
Built his heaven way beyond the stars.

### LEVI

Mouland.

### MOULAND

Come back among us, Lord.
That we may be at one with Thee–

### JESSOP

Here he comes now.
The Lord God of Levi.
Sword in hand, reins in his teeth,
Legs astride the blood red beast wit' two horns blazin'.

*MOULAND gaffs JESSOP, hook in collar, drags him onto the block of ice.*

### MOULAND

You thinks you can put things right, killing what you don't like.
Is that it Jessop? Answer me!

*MOULAND forces JESSOP to his knees, then face down.*

### MOULAND

Answer me!

*JESSOP attempts to rise. MOULAND pins him underfoot, raises the gaff to strike.*

### MOULAND

I'm goin' home to my Belle.

### MCCARTHY

Art, b'y. We needs yer gaff fer the young swile.

### MOULAND

Wha...?

*MCCARTHY exits with the gaff. JESSOP hands MOULAND the knife.*

**JESSOP**

Save yer skin, Mouland.
Go on b'y. Go home to yer wife and child.
I can't tell the difference between mine and the swile pup's no more.

*MOULAND raises JESSOP's head, exposing his throat. They are washed with flickering light; aurora borealis.*

**LEVI**

The gates of heaven open to receive our souls.
God help me.
Am I to enter heaven a broken man?

*The harmonic tones, rise – pure, sustained.*

**MOULAND**

The spirits of the dead men leaves their bodies, look!

**LEVI**

They rises, drawn upwards to the blessed face of God.
See how their souls flickers with joy as they rises up.

**MOULAND**

Shimmers on the new ice below...

**JESSOP**

No! That's never the joy of man.
That's the spirits of the seals.
See how they flickers back to life,
Scuttles across the pans and pitches back into the sea.

*MOULAND brings the knife to JESSOP's throat. LEVI stays MOULAND's hand.*

**LEVI**

Tell me about hard-hearted fathers and ungrateful sons now.

*COLLINS enters.*

**COLLINS**

Art! McCarthy's killin' the seal! I needs yer knife.

*MOULAND gives COLLINS the knife. COLLINS exits.*

**JESSOP**

Red sky in morning, sealer take warning.

**LEVI**

The sun is rising Jessop. Ye'll never see it set.

**TUFF**

(*off*)
Raise the gaff above the young seal's head.
Bring it down with all your force.

*JESSOP slumps.*

**TUFF**

(*off*)
Good.

*LEVI resumes his place between ANDREW and SIMON.*

**LEVI**

Come on, me sons. There's no more fish in these waters.
We're goin' home.

*Silence. Stillness. A wash of morning light. COLLINS enters.*

**COLLINS**

Art, b'y. We got the seal.
There's food, Skipper. There's heat. There's blood.
Look...

*MCCARTHY enters, towing the opened carcass. TUFF follows.
MOULAND moves to them, stumbles.*

**COLLINS**

Get to your feet, Skipper Art. Come on. That's the way.

**TUFF**

Put me onto the carcass.

*MCCARTHY guides TUFF down to the seal. TUFF drinks heavily*

**MCCARTHY**

That's enough, George. George! That's enough!

**COLLINS**

Art. Tuff's hoggin' it all to hisself.

**MOULAND**

Tuff. Give over. Ye'll sicken yourself.
(*hauls TUFF off*)
Lem. Yer molasses can. Give it here.

*MOULAND fills the can with blood, hands it to MCCARTHY.*

**MOULAND**

Take a glutch. Just a swally. Roll it around in yer mouth. Spit out.
Take a little more. Glutch 'er down. Good.

**COLLINS**

Skipper. Drink.

**MOULAND**

After ye.

> *COLLINS drinks. MOULAND tries to rouse JESSOP.*

Jessop. Drink. Just a little.

**JESSOP**

(*drinks*)
It's bitter. It's sweet.

**MOULAND**

Take a little more.

> *JESSOP pushes the can away. MOULAND drinks, spits, drinks again.*

Lemuel. Hand me the young swile's heart.
(*to JESSOP*)
I'll cut the heart abroad and give it to the men.

> *COLLINS extracts the pup's heart, holds it momentarily, hands it to
> MOULAND.*

**COLLINS**

Such heat.

**MCCARTHY**

Put your hands back inside the carcass to thaw, Lem.
Lest you lose them fingers.

> *MOULAND sits with JESSOP, slices strips from the heart. He attempts
> to feed JESSOP.*

**MOULAND**

Come on Jessop. Sit up, now.
Ye might as well eat the meat as drink the gravy.

**MCCARTHY**

Art, b'y–

**MOULAND**

Don't be obstinate. You got to eat to live.

**MCCARTHY**

You're too late.

**MOULAND**

Please, Jessop.

**MCCARTHY**

He's gone.

> *The dead sealers disperse, or ease themselves back down to the ice. TUFF falls, trembles, lies still.*

**MOULAND**

George Tuff. Get to yer feet.

**TUFF**

Look!

**MOULAND**

What?

**TUFF**

The teeth. The terrible teeth.
And oh! The eyes of blood and fire.

**MOULAND**

(*straddles TUFF*)
I'll slit yer guts wide open like Richard done that seal
If ye don't get to yer feet.

> *TUFF rolls on his side and vomits. He sits up.*

**TUFF**

God forgive me. I took too much.

> *Low in the background, the rev of engines.*

**COLLINS**

Skipper George.

**TUFF**

What?

**COLLINS**

Skipper George! Come here.

#### TUFF
Where are ye to?

#### COLLINS
Here. Along side 'a Tom Dawson.

*Ship's engine present.*

#### COLLINS
Last time ye seen him, was he lyin' on his right side or his left?

#### TUFF
What difference does it make now?

#### COLLINS
Maybe all the difference in the world. Right or left?

#### TUFF
Left.

#### COLLINS
He's lyin' on his right side now.

#### TUFF
(*makes his way to COLLINS*)
Where is he?

#### COLLINS
At yer feet.

#### TUFF
(*feels DAWSON's face*)
He's still warm. Tom. Can ye hear me?

*DAWSON groans.*

#### TUFF
Lem. Bring the blood. Tom, b'y. Set up.

#### DAWSON
I'm froze to the ice.

#### TUFF
Drink this.

#### DAWSON
Me hands is gone.

*TUFF holds the can. DAWSON drinks.*

**TUFF**

Easy does it. Slosh it around yer mouth.
Spit it out. Now a little more. Swally it.

*A moment. DAWSON bellows, raises his torso with force.*

**DAWSON**

Billy?

**MOULAND**

Gone, b'y.
Gone home.

*Engines increase in volume. Ship's whistle. Three sharp blasts.*

**COLLINS**

Smoke. Close to hand, nor' west.

**MOULAND**

B'ys. Help me up.

*MOULAND climbs the pinnacle. He waves. A moment. He waves again.*

**MOULAND**

They seen me.

**TUFF**

Are ye sure?

**MOULAND**

They returned me wave twice.

**MCCARTHY**

Hail, Holy Queen, mother of mercy.
Hail our life, our sweetness and our hope.

**DAWSON**

Free me from the ice.
Stop. Stop!
My feet, b'ys. I lost them too.

**TUFF**

I'll stay beside ye.

**DAWSON**

Stay beside me!
Do ye want to be found huddled like a crowd of gutless wonders?
Or walk aboard of the ship, like men and Newfoundlanders?

**TUFF**

I don't know what'd happen if I had to report
I'd lost the strongest man on the ice.

**DAWSON**

Tell them where I'm to and leave me be.
Set about yer business, Tuff.

> *Ship's whistle. Enter Captain Abram KEAN, clad head to foot in*
> *luxurious, tailored sealskin garments.*

**KEAN**

Who are they?

**MOULAND**

Levi Templeman.
His two son's Andrew and Simon.

**KEAN**

Levi had three sons. Where's Jessop?

> *MOULAND indicates JESSOP's body.*

Why is he not with his brothers?

**MOULAND**

I couldn't say.

**KEAN**

Great sealers, the Templemans.
I wish it was all Templemans.
You've made a bad job of it Tuff.
A very bad job indeed.

**TUFF**

It wasn't me sold the men that damn American underwear.

**KEAN**

What're ye on about?

**TUFF**

I believe the men wearing wool lived.

**KEAN**

Why didn't ye make for yer own ship, as I instructed?

**TUFF**

I lost the trail.

**COLLINS**

We lost the trail. In the starm.

**KEAN**

You leave a ship wit' a 'undred and thirty two men, Tuff,
Ye return wit' a 'undred and thirty two men.

**TUFF**

You're going to try to pin this on me, ain't ye?

**KEAN**

You there.

**OFFICER**

Yes, Captain?

**KEAN**

Get these poor souls a blanket and a cup of tea.
And send a wire to Captain Randall on the *SS Bellaventure* yonder.
Tell him to rendezvous here to pick up the *Newfoundland*'s crew.
Wire the *Nascopie*, *The Eagle*. Tell them to collect the living and dead,
And take them to the *Belle*. Randall's got a full load of fat.
He can take them back to St. John's wit' him.
Tell them to make it snappy. And tell Randall to keep me informed.

**OFFICER**

Yes sir.

**TUFF**

I can't be blamed for the wet fellas.

**KEAN**

That will do, Tuff. Go aboard.

**TUFF**

Leave me be, Lem.
I took me last order from Captain Abram Kean.
I'll wait for Captain Randall.

*DAWSON is loaded on a stretcher.*

**DAWSON**

Be careful of me feet. God help me. Me hands is gone too.

**KEAN**

Frost bite, is it? Ye'll be good as new in a day or two.

**DAWSON**

I'll never be good as new ye cripplin' old son of a bitch.

**KEAN**

Get this man aboard. Put him in the hold.

**DAWSON**

You'll not stuff me in yer stinkin' hold.
I'll stay on deck 'till St John's town for all the world to see.

**KEAN**

Suit yerself.

      *Dawson is carried off.*

**MOULAND**

You're the blind Barrel Man. How is it you never seen us?

**BARREL MAN**

I passed me glass over this quare patch of seals lyin' around on the ice.
I couldn't make sense of their antics. I never thought ye was men.
How did ye live?

**MOULAND**

I portioned out my strength.

**KEAN**

How many is lost?

**MOULAND**

Too many. How many dead, Richard?

**MCCARTHY**

I'd say well over half the men have perished.

**KEAN**

There's a Second Hand's job available, Mouland.
Starting as of now. What do ye say?

**MOULAND**

First I'll see to my men. Livin' and dead.
Once aboard of the *Newfoundland*, I'll report to Captain Wes.
Then I'll take some soup.
One bowl. That's all.
I'll sleep for four hours, neither more or less.

I'll rise and eat a large meal.
I'll stand as Master Watch aboard of the *Newfoundland*,
As I have done these last five springs.
Once ashore, I'll greet my wife and child.
If asked, I'll speak the truth as I seen it.

### KEAN

How's that?

### MOULAND

We should never have been put on the ice in a storm in the first place.

*KEAN shifts his attention to the ice.*

### KEAN

There's seals to be 'arvested, Mouland.
Report to yer vessel.
Tuff. See to your dead.

*KEAN exits. The voices of men cry out in the distance. Harp cows call for their pups. Ice cracks.*

### MOULAND

Belle? I knows what I seen in yer eyes that night in St John's town.
I seen God. I seen God this very night.
Not Levi's God of trial and retribution.
Or the merchant's God of power, greed and fear.
I seen a constant God, a tender God whose blessed name is Love.
I will stand by your side for as long as you will have me.
I will take delight in the spirits of our children.
I will love you – I will praise your name – forever.
Belle, my dear... I'm coming home.

*The* Stephano's *whistle sounds. Her engines roar. Black smoke billows.*

*The end.*

"Richard Rose, back to camera, Stages the curtain call. Captain Art Andrew's two masted island trader, right, appeared as the rescue ship the SS Stephano, in the final scene of the play."

## PLAYWRIGHT'S NOTE: AFTER WORDS

> *The deep down dirty secret of dramatic writing is that it is poetry.*
> *That's what makes a play work in addition to the plot.*
> — DAVID MAMET, Playwright/Screenwriter.

I hadn't yet encountered David Mamet's compact quote when I undertook the research and writing of this mammoth project in 1994. It was 1998, opening night, before my own personal "eureka."

When Donna Butt asked me to propose a subject she might commission for Rising Tide, I undertook the research for *The Harps of God*, a tragedy in three acts for twenty men, determined to be faithful to the survivors accounts of *The Great Newfoundland Sealing Disaster of 1914*, recorded in two commissions of enquiry. It became apparent that the facts were shrouded; honourable men speak no ill of the dead. After the loss of a father and all his sons, a family's good name is its only legacy. The friend who survives does not betray by revealing behaviour uncharacteristic of his friend who did not. It was not my task to attempt a faithful historical re-enactment of this horrendous, heroic event. Nor could I faithfully reconstruct the survivors, all gone now, unable to corroborate or elaborate. How does one honourably animate the dead? Instinct and circumstance propelled me to the realm of the mytho-poetic.

At the time, theatre in Canada was lost in it's own bleak landscape, not as harsh an environment as the ice fields of the North Atlantic in a March gale perhaps, but no less discouraging. Small plays, more naturally aligned to popular television writing than the great classics of the world theatrical repertoire, were pretty much guaranteed a place on Canadian stages. It seemed beleaguered Artistic Directors could convince box office driven boards of directors—too often comprised of experts in drama drawn from legal, medical and mercantile domains—that Canadian theatre was worthy of little more.

I had tired of writing five character works. I needed to "talk big." Attempts at epic drama were prohibited by default, hence Canada's best stories could not be told, for ours is a great sprawling history in a great and sprawling land. A big unwieldy play, a story from a region, not Toronto? A classically constructed tragedy for twenty men? In three acts? In Canada? In 1994?

Well, yes. If the producing theatre company is Rising Tide Theatre, and the Artistic Director is Donna Butt. And yes again, with the Canada Council's generous support. The soul of Newfoundland is tragi-poetic. There is a profound connection with loss and hardship, so eloquently articulated in Donna's Introduction to this edition. There is also a terrible, admirable will to survive on this rock in the North Atlantic pounded by the sea under a hard, hard climate.

It is said that a failure in communication is essential to all tragedy. Eighty of one hundred and twenty men died, standing, lying on their sides, seated taking off a boot, all hard as marble to save five dollars, the cost of a Marconi, and operator for the season. The urge to discover, then communicate, something of what the sealers of "old wooden walled" *S. S. Newfoundland* endured, of the courage, vision and self-sacrifice that makes some men gods when others remain monsters, remains at the heart of *The Harps of God*.

Theatre is first and foremost a collaborative art. I sought the best, and the best responded. I remembered the days when the National Arts Centre (NAC) in Ottawa toured great Canadian shows to this vast country's regions. Andis Celms, Artistic Director of English Theatre at the NAC came aboard. I was delighted. An article by Peter Smith in the Playwright's Workshop Montreal newsletter attracted the attention of Canada's foremost director, Richard Rose. I sent him an early draft. He responded positively. I was elated. Candace Burley, with her great heart and superb theatrical instincts was Head Dramaturg at Canadian Stage in Toronto at the time. She, together with Artistic Director Bob Baker, joined Rising Tide and The NAC in the development process and the future of *The Harps of God* was secured.

Is there a place in the northern hemisphere more beautiful than the town of Trinity on Trinity Bay, Newfoundland? The photos included with the text give a sense of the majesty of the setting. What the photos don't reveal is this: *Harps* was performed within sixty miles of the actual disaster site, with superb Newfoundland actors, many profoundly connected by heritage, and in their daily lives, to the seal fishery. When Dennis Hookey mimed the sculping of a seal carcass, deftly removing hide and three inch layer of fat in real time, we knew we were in the presence of something authentic, honourable, something linked to the survival of Newfoundland fishermen and their families that animal rights activists will never fully grasp.

Richard Rose's vivid description of opening night in his Preface stimulates a memory. The play was staged on the tumbled concrete foundation of a turn-of-the-century whaling station. Richard had set five powerful halogen lamps, two at ground level, three at about eye level, to light the play. As evening dissolved to a dusk of light rain and mist, the play also moved from day to night; a pool of light, white concrete blocks, the ice fields in the wet black surround, and beyond that across the bay lost in dense fog, Trinity.

The final scene, the rescue, was played down the steep slope of Maggoty Bay, on the shore. A ship emerges from the fog, her masts caught in the near distance by the same five lights. She docks, silently. The audience is ushered to the edge, where a clear view of the action is assured, about twenty metres below eye level, and perhaps thirty metres distant as the dead are collected, the survivors tended.

I lingered behind the audience and was startled by a vision that captured all I had attempted, a kind of phantom which rendered hope visible. The clear, powerful arc lights cast the shadows of the audience metres deep into the fog. Like a Victorian cutout silhouette, their shadows—their "shades"—hang carved in the mist, above the actors playing out the denouement below. The present hovered, floating above the past.

The poetry of performance, the beauty and power of landscape; intelligent, passionate direction and great vision; the hard work of wonderful collaborators; the struggle to achieve theatrical metaphor; the souls of the dead evoked by their offspring; where else but Newfoundland could such a vision arise? Who other than Donna Butt at Rising Tide Theatre, in the town of Trinity on Trinity Bay, could nurture such revelation?

E. K. S.
Montreal
March 24, 2001

On deck of a Ship

Two of Cap'n Kean's
"master watches,"
or gang captains.
(With men like these
to boss gangs, much
can be accomplished)

(From "Vikings of
the Ice.")

A42-138

## SHIP'S LOG: *S. S. FOGOTA*

The Front, 1914
Excerpts

**March 28th, 1914.** Weather fair and bright, ice fairly loose, picking up scattered seals all day, *S. S. EAGLE* in sight 3PM. *S. S. BEOTHIC* also, *NASCOPIE*, tied up for the night broad side. Capt. of the *S .S. FOGOTA*, steward and myself went on board to *S. S. NASCOPIE*, she has up-to-date 15,000. Returned 11:30, fixed up the sick, blind and cut, turned in 1:30AM.

**March 29th, 1914.** Sunday blowing a full gale all day wind N. W. and drifting snow all afternoon, a good swell in the ice and broken up, saw several smokes of other ships this afternoon too far to distinguish one from the other, also could see a few live seals and hundreds of carcasses from the barrel. This is Sunday and scarcely could get a drop of water to drink every person keeping Sunday, I had to get ice myself and melt for cleansing the cut hands, men that should do this spent it in their berths.... Chief engineer and his staff have been working all day his engine doing little, I was down giving him a hand, we cannot keep Sunday in our berths. John Rowe on the mend, fixed up the men's eyes that needed it in all twice today dressed Bridgemaster Powell's hand it is doing nicely again, also one deckhand with a gathered hand lanced it today, and 15 with cut hands washed them in antiseptic solution and put clean bandages on them, turned in 11PM barometer going down it is blowing hard and drifting.

**March 30th, 1914.** Light wind N. W. and clear a good swell in the ice all broken up but very tight we are making little progress took on board 30 seals. *EAGLE, NASCOPIE, SAGONA, BLOODHOUND* and *BEOTHIC* all here in sight. Seals very scarce our coal supply is getting short, our Chief Engineer figures about 80 tons of seal pelts now aboard. Attended the sick, and dressed cut hands, disinfected the ship forward and aft, and turned in at 11PM.

**Funk Islands, March 31st, 1914.** Before noon fine and clear good swell in the ice all broken up and very tight, we are making very little progress, we steamed about five miles all day and running the engine full speed, several of the ships seen yesterday still in sight, seals very scarce killed 37 in all. This afternoon drifting snow and blowing, picked up a lone flag but no seals, two hours picked up a pan with no flag but 97 seals on it, flag and this pan belong to the *S. S. FLORIZEL*, pan broken in several pieces, and several of the seal sculps gone into the water. Took what was left of them on board, still blowing and drifting, the ice jammed tight, 8PM. Funks off our Bow. Sick list: J. Rowe on the mend fast, he ate fairly well today, deck hand with gathered hand washed and poulticed it with Linseed meal. Also doing well. Nothing from the ice-blind today, this is a good sign. Several knife cuts washed and dressed. Nothing doing on the ice today, gave the ship a general clean up fore and aft, turned in 11PM.

**Atlantic Ocean, April 1st., 1914.** Wind N. W. Blowing a gale all day and drifting fierce, temperature zero (-18C), only two men on the ice this afternoon, they killed three seals each, the wind and drift let up for about an hour, and then started to blow harder than ever, I should judge the wind is blowing about 70 mile an hour. I was up and looked around before dark and noticed as did long before that the punts on the hurricane deck are not lashed down.... Why the way the wind is howling I wouldn't be surprised if some of the punts are blown overboard by morning. The sick the blind and the knife cuts are all doing well, turned in around 10PM.

**April 2nd, 1914.** N. W. Wind blowing hard and cold, all hands on ice 7:30AM ice jammed tight, *S. S. BLOODHOUND* the only ship in sight, *S. S. BOGOTA* did not move all day. Capt. took the sun noon and we now lay 58 miles off the Funk Island took 230 seals on board today, all hands on ice, I looked after the winenes and also helped engine room staff to get ice for domestic purposes. No sick list today all well fore and aft.

## SELECTED BIBLIOGRAPHY

*Magisterial Inquiry, 1914 Newfoundland Sealing Disaster*. April, 1914.

*Newfoundland Sealing Commission Inquiry into Facts Surrounding the Great Newfoundland Sealing Disaster of 1914*. November 1914 - January 1915.

*Old and Young Ahead (A Millionaire in Seals, Being the Life History of Captain Abram Kean, O.B.E.)* Abram Kean.

*Of Seals and Men*, James Candow.

*Man's Search For Meaning*, Viktor E. Frankl.

"The Book of Revelation" & "Psalm 51," *The Holy Bible*.

*Aspects of the Novel*, E.M. Forster.

*Death on the Ice*, Cassie Brown.

*The Art of Loving* and *You Shall Be As Gods*, Erich Fromm.

*The Tibetan Book of the Dead*, Traditional.

*William Coaker: A Biographical Sketch*, Donna Butt.

*Wake of the Great Sealers*, Farley Mowatt, David Blackwood.

*The Greatest Hunt in the World*, George A. England.

*Seals and Sealers*, Shannon Ryan.

*Haulin' Rope and Gaff*, Shannon Ryan, Larry Small.

*The Golden Bough*, J. G. Frazer.

*Messengers of God*, Elie Wiesel.

*photo: Steven Jack*

At first glance, writer/director Kent Stetson's view of the world seems a pretty straightforward blend of compassion and humor. A closer look reveals work that is lifted above the everyday by myth, irony and a delicious sense of the fantastic. Nothing is quite what it seems in Kent's work, yet everything makes absolute sense. Comedy, tragedy, and everything in between delight this versatile writer/director. His rural Prince Edward Island, Canada roots and current status as a Montrealler reflect his sensibilities to a tee.

Works include the widely produced drama, *Warm Wind in China* (Atlantis Films developed the feature screenplay), the black comedy *Queen of the Cadillac* (feature screenplay developed by Birdsong/Cadillac Productions). *The Harps of God*, a tragedy in three acts for twenty men, *The Eyes of the Gull*, a gothic romance and *Horse High, Bull Strong, Pig Tight* round out his repertoire.

Trained in television screen writing and directing by the British Broadcasting Corporation and the Canadian Broadcasting Corporation, Kent co-founded, wrote and directed for Charlottetown's independant film company Points East Productions, The National Film Board of Canada, CTV, and a wide variety of independent film companies.

Kent's work as a dramaturg has brought him to the National Theatre School of Canada, and Montreal's prestigious McGill and Concordia universities, where he has taught advanced playwrighting. He continues to write and direct for the theatre and screen, and offers his dramaturgical skills to the film community as script consultant/story editor.

# OTHER PLAYS
# BY KENT STETSON

## As I Am

## The Eyes of the Gull

## Horse High, Bull Strong, Pig Tight

## Just Plain Murder

## Queen of the Cadillac

## Sweet Magdalena

## Warm Wind in China

## Woodlot Rap
*(written with Wanda Graham)*

Available from Playwrights Union of Canada
416-703-0201    fax 703-0059
orders@puc.ca    http://www.puc.ca

*For more information about other works by*
*Kent Stetson, please visit his web site at:*
*www.MasterPlayWorks.com*

MEMBER OF SCABRINI MEDIA

Quebec, Canada
2002